Corn & Rat Snakes

Philip Purser

For Jenny

Corn & Rat Snakes

T.F.H. Publications
President/CEO: Glen S. Axelrod
Executive Vice President: Mark E. Johnson
Publisher: Christopher T. Reggio
Production Manager: Kathy Bontz

Project Team
Editor: Thomas Mazorlig
Copy Editor: Stephanie Fornino
Cover Design: Cándida Moreira Tómassini, Mary Ann Kahn
Design: Mary Ann Kahn

T.F.H. Publications, Inc.
One TFH Plaza
Third and Union Avenues
Neptune City, NJ 07753

Copyright © 2006 by T.F.H. Publications, Inc.

All rights reserved. No part of this publication may be reproduced, stored, or transmitted in any form, or by any means electronic, mechanical or otherwise, without written permission from T.F.H. Publications, except where permitted by law. Requests for permission or further information should be directed to the above address.

Printed and Bound in China
07 08 09   3 5 7 9 8 6 4 2
ISBN 978-0-79382880-7
Library of Congress Cataloging-in-Publication Data
Purser, Philip.. Corn snakes and rat snakes / a complete guide to pantherophis / Philip Purser.
p. cm.
Includes bibliographical references.
ISBN 0-7938-2880-5 (alk. paper)
1. Corn snakes as pets. 2. Rat snakes as pets. I. Title.
SF459.S5P86 2004
639.3'96--dc22
2005029664

This book has been published with the intent to provide accurate and authoritative information in regard to the subject matter within. While every precaution has been taken in preparation of this book, the author and publisher expressly disclaim responsibility for any errors, omissions, or adverse effects arising from the use or application of the information contained herein. The techniques and suggestions are used at the reader's discretion and are not to be considered a substitute for veterinary care. If you suspect a medical problem, consult your veterinarian.

The Leader In Responsible Animal Care For Over 50 Years!™
www.tfh.com

Table of Contents

Chapter 1

Understanding
Corn Snakes

What is a corn snake? While this may sound like a simple question, it's not so easy to answer. For starters, corn snakes belong to a group of snakes known as colubrids. Colubrids are typically long, slender, muscular snakes, and only a few of them are venomous. Colubrids come from all corners of the globe, save for Antarctica, and do not grow nearly as large as some of the boas and pythons. Colubrids are by far the most populous snakes in the world, and they compose over 75 percent of the 3,000 snakes species known to exist.

What's in a Name?

Some hobbyists suspect that the corn snake takes its common name from its frequent association with corncribs and farmyards. While corn snakes are often encountered in such places, it is most likely that these animals were so named because of their stunning coloration, which is highly reminiscent of the crisp red, yellow, and orange kernels on Indian corn. The Latin nomenclature first given to this species is *Elaphe guttata guttata*, which translates to "speckled and spotted deerskin," referring to both the corn snake's beautifully mottled coloration, and its fine, leathery-smooth scales.

More specifically than that, a corn snake is also a type of rat snake, which is known for its superior rodent-hunting abilities. The rat snakes first appear in the fossil record about 55 million years ago and are currently found in North America, Europe, and Asia. The corn snake, however, is strictly a North American creature. Conservative estimates calculate that the corn snake has existed in its present form for about 25 to 30 million years. Where corn snakes occur in North America, they typically occur in large numbers. They, like all rat snakes, are quite secretive, however, and their true numbers remain unknown.

Description

Found from New Jersey south through the Florida Keys and west through Illinois and the Mississippi River Valley, the corn snake varies in coloration and size throughout this range. In my home state of Georgia, for example, there are roughly three color varieties of corn snake. In the northern end of the state, these snakes wear a base coat of gray to lead or ashen with saddles of dark brown to rusty-tan and dorsolateral (between the side and the back) blotches of yellowish to orange. In eastern Georgia, the saddles and dorsolateral blotches are unchanged, yet the base color is rusty to brownish-orange. And when exploring in the southern end of the state, it's no rare thing to turn up a corn snake that is almost solid reddish orange, its saddles defined from its base color only by their black edges. The best known of all color phases, however, comes from South Carolina and is known as the Okeetee corn snake. Okeetee corn snakes have a deep orange-red base color accented with crisply black-edged dorsal saddles.

The belly of almost all corn snakes is a clean, checkerboard pattern of black and white squares, but it may be orange to yellowish and unchecked in those specimens occurring in extreme southern Florida.

To scientists who study snakes, the number and arrangement of scales on a snake is important in determining what species it belongs to. There are many snake species that look

There are several local varieties of the corn snake, including the intensely red Okeetee (bottom) and the silvery Miami phase (top).

similar but have different numbers and arrangements of scales. The scale details of the corn snake are pretty straightforward. The head is covered in nine groups of specialized scales called plates: two internasal scales, two prefrontal scales, one frontal scale, two supraocular scales, and two parietal scales. The dorsum is covered in 27 to 34 rows of scales that are weakly keeled. That is to say, each scale has a faint ridge, or keel, running through its center. The anal plate is divided.

The body itself is shaped like a loaf of bread, with a flat bottom, vertical sides, and a rounded top. This muscular design is what allows the corn snake to be such an accomplished climber. Like many snakes, the corn snake's muscles and scales are specially adapted for moving swiftly and gracefully through the treetops. Corn snakes are so agile, in fact, that they have been observed with their lower half wrapped tightly around a tree branch and their forequarters coiled into a striking loop, lashing out to snag bats on the wing.

Hunting and Prey

Within their ecosystem, corn snakes are accomplished predators that survive by preying upon any warm-blooded animal they can subdue. Mice, rats, chipmunks, voles, moles, shrews, and baby rabbits are all potential prey. Occasionally, corn snakes, especially hatchlings, will eat lizards. They may venture into treetops, barn lofts, attics, and even straight up brick walls in search of nesting birds or their eggs.

Corn snakes climb with the aid of specialized belly scales and powerful rib muscles. Very tough and rigid at their edges, these belly scales grip the bark of trees or the grout of a brick wall and allow the snake to venture well off the ground. All North American rat snakes climb in this fashion.

Corn snakes kill their prey by constriction. When prey comes close, the corn snake will strike out and bite onto the animal, which is held fast by the corn snake's curved teeth. In the next few seconds, the corn snake will loop itself around its prey several times and will begin to squeeze. It was originally thought that a corn snake crushed its prey, smashing its bones, but this is not true. Constriction puts tremendous pressure on the prey's internal systems and leads to suffocation. The lungs do not inhale, and whenever the prey tries to take a breath, the snake will tighten up. Eventually, the heart will stop beating. Constriction is a very efficient means of dispatching prey, as the corn snake expends minimal energy.

When it comes to the senses, corn snakes have a keen sense of smell. Situated in a cavity in the roof of the mouth, a sensory organ called Jacobson's organ registers the scent particles that adhere to that ever-flicking tongue. The organ detects any prey or mates that are in or have been in the area. It is widely accepted that a corn snake's olfactory sense is many times more acute than our own. Once a corn snake has smelled out its prey, it relies on its motion-sensitive vision to pinpoint the rodent or bird and direct its strike.

Corn Snakes as Pets

Corn snakes demand little in captivity and can thrive under the care of even the most inexperienced hobbyists. Thus, the corn snake makes an excellent choice for the younger

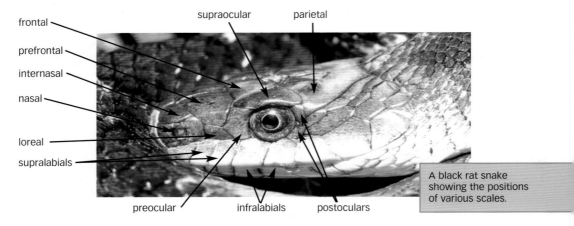

A black rat snake showing the positions of various scales.

Scale Terms

Many of the scales on a snake have names used by scientists and other professionals to facilitate discussions of snake anatomy, taxonomy, and other subjects. A partial glossary of these named scales is below.

anal: Scale that covers the vent. It is divided in the rat snakes.

frontal: Scale on top of the head, between the eyes. There is only one in the rat snakes.

infralabials: Scales on the lower "lip" (although snakes don't really have lips).

internasals: Scales on top of the head between the nostrils.

loreal: Scale on the side of the head between the nasal and the preoculars.

nasal: Scale on the side of the head surrounding (at least partially) the nostril

parietals: Scales on top of the head behind the frontal and supraoculars. Paired in rat snakes.

postocular: Scale or scales on the side of the head behind the eye.

prefrontals: Scales (two in rat snakes) on top of the head behind the internasals.

preoculars: Scales on the sides of the head in front of the eyes.

rostral: Scale on the tip of the snout.

subcaudals: Scales on the undersurface of the tail. Males have more than females.

supralabials: Scales on the upper "lip."

surpacoulars: Scales directly above the eye.

ventrals: Scales on the belly.

hobbyist or the novice wishing to try his or her hand at snake keeping for the first time. Delightfully mild-mannered, corn snakes are also frequently used by zoos, state parks, and nature centers as demonstration animals. Lying quietly coiled while a horde of curious children stroke its smooth skin, a frequently displayed corn snake rarely, if ever, shows any signs of aggression, and it is one of the most easily handled of all snakes.

A great many snake keepers complain of their pets not feeding well. Refusal of food in captivity can become a serious problem for many species of snakes, but as can be expected, this is seldom a problem with corn snakes. From the day they hatch until the day they pass into that big Terrarium in the Sky, captive corn snakes feed willingly and heartily on just about any warm-blooded morsel to cross their path. Even accepting frozen/thawed feeders as if they

Corn snakes and the other rat snakes are all adept climbers. Most rat snakes will prey on birds and bird eggs.

were fresh, the corn snakes can make feeding time extremely easy. In fact, more effort will go into fixing your own dinner than fixing the dinner of your corn snake.

Corn snakes are long-lived animals. With a record longevity of just over 32 years, a captive corn snake can indeed be a long-term companion. Purchasing a corn snake as a pet is a major decision that should not be taken lightly or conducted on a whim. These animals can easily bring years of enjoyment to their keeper, but they deserve devotion and commitment from their keeper in return.

Growth and Life Span

Because the purchase of a pet is a big decision that carries long-term responsibilities, it is critical for the hobbyist to understand just how fast that pet will grow, how big it will grow, and how long it will live. Just imagine the shock of a hobbyist who purchased a baby reticulated python on a whim, and only after the fact learned that this is the largest snake species in the world, and it can grow to well over 20 feet (6.1m) long!

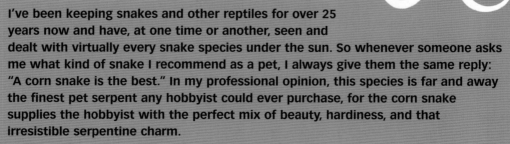

The Best Pet Snake

I've been keeping snakes and other reptiles for over 25 years now and have, at one time or another, seen and dealt with virtually every snake species under the sun. So whenever someone asks me what kind of snake I recommend as a pet, I always give them the same reply: "A corn snake is the best." In my professional opinion, this species is far and away the finest pet serpent any hobbyist could ever purchase, for the corn snake supplies the hobbyist with the perfect mix of beauty, hardiness, and that irresistible serpentine charm.

Fortunately, corn snakes remain a manageable size throughout their life. The smallest adults (those animals from extreme southern Florida) may not exceed 30 to 36 inches (76.2 to 91.4 cm) long, while even the largest corn snakes, those native to the Mid-Atlantic states, seldom attain 74 inches (188 cm) in length. Corn snakes are also sleek, streamlined animals, so even a very large corn snake, when coiled, can easily be held in an adult's open palms. The corn snake's modest stature makes it an attractive choice for children and hobbyists who have limited space to dedicate to their pets. This species' small size also ensures that the corn snake will never require monstrous-sized meals, like rabbits or guinea pigs, which can be quite expensive.

With its manageable size, undemanding requirements, docile temperament, and stunning beauty, the corn snake may be the very best pet snake.

Despite the fact that they stay relatively small in size, corn snakes—if well fed—will grow at impressively fast rates. Hatchling corn snakes have an efficient metabolism and can convert roughly one-third of their food into body mass. As an example, if a hatchling consumes 9 ounces (255 g) of food, it will add 3 ounces (85 g) of body weight. Growth in terms of length is also quite rapid. A 10-inch (25.4 cm) hatchling may grow to nearly 40 inches (101.6 cm) long in an 18- to 24-month period. Of course, it is during the corn snake's first two years of life that it grows so rapidly—it will slow down drastically thereafter. A 40-inch-long (101.6 cm), two-year-old snake may only add another 20 to 25 inches (50.8 to 63.5 cm) (or less) in length over the next three to five years of its life. While the growth rate in late adulthood may be minuscule, these serpents will continue to grow throughout their entire lives; even very old individuals may add a centimeter or two in length over several years.

Speaking of age, it's important to note that corn snakes can live for a very long time. The longest life span I've personally ever encountered was just under 31 years, though reports of

Scientific Names

You may have noticed that sometimes there are words in italics that appear after the name of an animal. This is the scientific name, and each animal only has one scientific name. Biologists determine the scientific name of each animal based on what other animals it is related to. Each scientific name has two parts: The first part of the name is called the genus, while the second part is the species. This combination of genus and species is unique for each animal. Scientific names allow scientists all over the world to talk about each animal without worrying about language barriers or other similar animals being confused with the one they want to discuss.

A scientific name is often abbreviated after the first usage. The genus is abbreviated to the first letter. So, after introducing the corn snake as *Pantherophis guttatus,* it can be referred to as *P. guttatus*. If the author is talking about all the rat snakes in this genus, he or she can use *Pantherophis* without a species name attached. Some animals have a third name, which indicates that it is a subspecies. Subspecies describe different varieties that exist within a species.

slightly older specimens do exist. This is not the average age, however. Healthy, well-kept individuals commonly reach the 20- to 25-year-old range. So if you're 20 years old when you buy a hatchling corn snake, and you take good care of it, you can expect it to be with you until you are in your mid-40's!

To ensure the best, most rewarding, and most long-term experience in the field of corn snake keeping, I advise any hobbyist to purchase an animal that has been bred in captivity and which is between three to six months old at the time of purchase. Purchasing such an animal will allow you to see your new pet grow and mature through its various stages of life, while at the same time granting you as many years as possible to enjoy your beautiful new corn snake. Additionally, a snake of this age won't be a delicate hatchling in need of tiny prey items.

The Name Game

Within the pages of this book, I will refer to the corn snake solely as *Pantherophis guttatus guttatus*. Any newcomers to the hobby will recognize this Latin name and shouldn't have any problems. To veteran hobbyists, however, this new and radically different nomenclature may be a little harder to swallow.

Please commit to your pet corn snake for it's entire life—perhaps as long as 30 years. A striped corn snake is shown.

The corn snake has been known as *Elaphe guttata* since 1833, when the genus was first described. (Prior to this, the corn snake was called *Coluber guttatus*.) That's over 170 years worth of nomenclature that is no longer universally recognized. In 2002, an article came to light that convinced many scientists, hobbyists, and professional breeders that a change of name was in order. Though it certainly came as a shock to a great many snake lovers, there are scientifically grounded reasons for this change of name.

In the *Russian Journal of Herpetology*, Urs Utiger and his team announced their findings that the North American *Elaphe* rat snakes are not closely related to their European and Asian *Elaphe* counterparts. Their conclusion is that all North American species should no longer be recognized as belonging to *Elaphe*. Instead, they resurrect an older form, *Pantherophis*, to designate the North American species. The name change would not affect those species belonging to the genera of *Bogertophis* and *Senticolis*, which are also North American rat snakes.

Bear in mind that these changes to nomenclature are not written in stone, and the hobbyist is free to decide which system of nomenclature he or she prefers. Remember that all literature, articles, books, etc. written prior to 2002 will always refer to these North American rat snakes as *Elaphe*. No matter what name is more accurate, it is best that interested hobbyists be familiar with both the established and the new systems of classification where these serpents are concerned.

Corn Snake Subspecies

There are currently two naturally occurring subspecies of corn snake recognized. These are the corn snake, *Pantherophis guttatus guttatus*, and the Great Plains rat snake, *Pantherophis guttatus emoryi*, which is found west of the Mississippi River. Note that some consider the Great Plains rat snake a separate species under the name *Pantherophis emoryi*. These subspecies, as well as all other North American rat snakes, are discussed in greater detail in Chapter 8.

Chapter 2

The Corn Snake Terrarium

Transit from the breeder, to the pet shop, to your house is stressful enough, without the corn snake having to spend three or four hours waiting around in a dark box or pillowcase while you construct its new habitat. Purchasing the materials and setting up your corn snake's new home before purchasing the animal itself is a cardinal rule of corn snake husbandry. Even if it will be living in a quarantine tank for the first few weeks, any new addition to your serpent collection deserves a warm, safe, and secure place to live from the moment it arrives at your home.

Caging

Because corn snakes do not attain the tremendous lengths that some snakes do, one individual snake may live its entire life in a terrarium no bigger than 75 gallons (284 l). Of course, you'll want to offer your animal as much room as you can throughout its life, because a corn snake that is constantly held in cramped quarters is likely to be stressed.

A good rule of thumb is to offer your corn snake a terrarium in which it can fully stretch out, with no part of it touching the glass. A 30-inch-long (76.2 cm) snake, for example, might do well in a tank that is at least 36 inches (91.4 cm) long. Width and height are also major concerns, as these snakes are natural climbers, and a terrarium that is too low will not allow them to use the vertical space that a taller tank will supply. If you have the room, a 72-inch-long by 24-inch-tall (183 by 61 cm) glass terrarium (roughly 125 gallons, or 473 liters) will provide a single corn snake or a pair of corn snakes all the room they will ever need in captivity. To the snake living in such spacious quarters, it may seem as if it is not in captivity at all.

Of course, not all hobbyists use glass aquarium style tanks to house their pet snakes. The wave of the future is the acrylic (sometimes called molded plastic) herp-specific terrarium. These light-weight, highly durable tanks have been evolving for several years now, and it seems that a new and better style hits the market every time you can turn around. The best of these acrylic terraria are not so much single tanks as they are individual components in a larger network of

> With the addition of a heat source and a secure cage top, this aquarium will make a suitable home for this snow corn snake.

terraria; each is stackable and interlocks with other tanks designed to fit it.

Acrylic terraria are constructed out of highly durable, heat and chemical resistant polyethylene. The sides and back of some models are opaque, though fully transparent models are also common. These tanks are lightweight (much lighter than a glass tank of equivalent volume) and have molded holes and grooves to readily accommodate light and heater attachments; some models even have a light shroud built-in. The front is generally composed of clear sliding glass or acrylic doors. Most models come with locks. Of course, all this convenience and technology comes at a much higher price than a good old glass terrarium.

Acrylic shoeboxes are often used by hobbyists and breeders to house hatchling and juvenile snakes.

If you've been around the hobby for a while, you've undoubtedly heard someone talking about the sweater boxes or shoe boxes in which they house their snakes. Available in most department stores and hardware stores, these plastic boxes are lightweight and come fitted with appropriate lids. They cost much less than the other housing options. While most folks fill these boxes with winter clothes and old shoes, we hobbyists know how to quickly and easily convert these items into low-cost herp-homes. Simply drill or melt a series of small holes into the sides or lid of the box for ventilation, slap an undertank heating pad on one end of the bottom, and securely fasten the lid to the top, and voila, you've just constructed a tough, durable, and above all inexpensive home for your corn snake. Some pet supply companies have started manufacturing versions of these boxes with the air holes predrilled. While many species of herps would stress or suffer when housed in such a simple enclosure, the easily kept corn snake doesn't seem to mind such accommodations, just so long as it's taken out and exercised regularly.

Substrate

Once you have picked out the enclosure in which your new corn snake will live, you must decide what type of substrate to use. Don't let the word *substrate* fool you. It may sound like something complicated, but *substrate* is just another way of saying *flooring* or *bedding* material.

There are two major schools of thought when it comes to substrate: natural and artificial. Each of these varieties has its pros and cons, and each can be perfectly suitable to the long-term housing of one or more corn snakes.

Natural Substrates

A natural substrate is just that—natural—and can be made of coconut husks, bark chips, mulch, etc. Natural substrate is similar to what wild corn snakes are accustomed to, and just about any corn snake will thrive on natural bedding, as long as the substrate is not kept overly wet. In my opinion, a blend of several natural substrates gives the terrarium a very naturalistic appearance and is best all around. I suggest mixing some reptile bark-style bedding with shredded coconut husks, both of which may be purchased at most pet shops dealing in reptiles and amphibians. Layer the mixture at least 3 inches (7.6 cm) deep. Since some corn snakes like to burrow, this depth of bedding will allow yours to do so.

The drawbacks to natural substrates are that they are more difficult to clean, may hold excess moisture, may harbor bacteria, and typically hide expelled wastes. Natural substrates also tend to be more expensive than some artificial substrates.

No Carpets for Corn Snakes

Some hobbyists cut a square of indoor/outdoor carpet to fit their terrarium. I advise against using carpet, however, because its nylon threads can become tangled around corn snakes, especially juveniles, and may constrict the blood flow. Additionally, it is difficult to get this substrate clean.

Artificial Substrates

Artificial substrates are easier than natural ones when it comes to clean-up time. Newspaper, plain white paper towels, recycled newspaper bedding, or pelleted bedding, which may be sold as "lizard litter," are all excellent choices.

Most artificial substrates absorb odors, hold little moisture, and once soiled, are easily thrown out and replaced. Sick or ailing corn snakes are best housed on several layers of soft paper towels, as this substrate allows the animal to be most easily viewed during this period of recovery and observation. The major drawbacks to the artificial substrates are mostly aesthetics. It just isn't too impressive to see a 5-foot-long (1.5 m) Okeetee corn snake lying coiled on a copy of the Sunday newspaper.

Substrates to Avoid

Whichever style of substrate you decide to employ, there are some that must avoided at all costs. Excessively rough or jagged stones, such as lava rock, can nick, cut, scrape, or otherwise seriously abrade your corn snake. Pine or cedar shavings must *never* be used. Corn snakes have a very acute sense of smell, and the oils and heavy resins in pine and cedar shavings can seriously irritate the corn snake's olfactory glands. Prolonged exposure to such substrates can cause permanent, irreversible damage to your corn snake. I also advise against using a substrate of small aquarium pebbles or sand, as these items may be ingested along with a meal and may become impacted in the corn snake's gut. They also allow wastes to sink beneath them, resulting in a bacterial breeding ground.

A Baird's rat snake housed on recycled newspaper bedding. This substrate is becoming more popular with hobbyists and breeders

A final substrate to avoid is printed paper towels. The dyes used to print paper towels are often caustic or irritating, and over a period of prolonged exposure, these agents can cause mild to serious troubles in your corn snake's skin and scales.

Furnishings and Decorations

Choosing the furnishings of your corn snake's cage is much like choosing the substrate. You may opt for natural environs, which are aesthetically much more pleasing, or you may choose artificial furnishings, which are much easier to clean. Natural items may include large stones, slabs of driftwood, Spanish moss tangles, climbing branches, pinecones, hollow logs, or anything else along those lines. Many natural items are available from your local pet shop and have been cleaned before being packaged. This treatment is important, as items brought into the terrarium from the wild often harbor some type of parasite, fungus, or bacteria. Though in nature they pose little threat, in the captive environment, these tiny organisms can present problems to your corn snake in the form of infection or serious irritation.

Treat any and all items you may gather from the wild before introducing them into the terrarium. By using the following "recipe" for treatment, you can decontaminate any such items in your own home:

Eliminate the Undesirables

Untreated natural décor or substrate from the outdoors will likely harbor molds, fungi, and a host of parasites. Always heat-treat any natural furnishings before putting them into your corn or rat snake's terrarium.

1. Wrap all natural items in aluminum foil.
2. Place them in the oven.
3. Set the oven to 250° F (121.1°C).
4. Let the items bake for 45-65 minutes.
5. Allow the items to cool for 4-6 hours before putting them in the terrarium.

Baking all gathered wood, brick, stone, etc. at 250°F (121.1°C) (which is not hot enough to actually burn your wooden items) will ensure that most microorganisms inhabiting those items will be destroyed. If you have an item that is too large to fit into the oven, wash it thoroughly with very hot water and allow it to dry in the sun for a couple of days before placing it in the terrarium.

Organize the terrarium however you like or in a way that your corn snake seems to enjoy. Remember that your snake will need one or more sturdy climbing branches and will relish both open ground, as well as areas of dense cover. For example, a hiding box and a climbing branch situated toward one end of the terrarium with an open area toward the other end will provide the corn snake with a diverse habitat. Too much open area or too much clutter in a terrarium can be stressful to your corn snake.

Plants

Many hobbyists consider putting live plants in their corn snake terrarium. While living plants may be attractive, I must professionally advise against them. Not only can living plants not be heat-treated against harmful microorganisms, but the movements of an adult corn snake can grind down and destroy even the most robust of houseplants in a matter of days.

Artificial plants, on the other hand, can be a herpetological godsend. Sturdy, attractive, and easily cleaned, plastic plants come in a wide variety of sizes, shapes, and colors to suit any hobbyist's taste. Some even come with suction cup attachments and adhere to the walls of your terrarium, allowing you to place them virtually anywhere. A climbing branch with a dense cluster of artificial vegetation at the top may soon become your corn snake's favorite retreat, as it simulates what the corn snake would encounter in nature. Artificial ferns, vines, and other broadleaf plants can add a definite element of seclusion and naturalism to your terrarium.

Hides

Adequate hides are an integral part of any corn snake terrarium. In the wild, corn snakes survive by hiding from would-be predators and feel exposed, endangered, and severely stressed when they cannot find a dark, tight-fitting shelter into which they can retreat. A wild corn snake that cannot hide stands little chance of survival, and your captive pet will not forget over 25 million years of instinct simply because it is in the terrarium.

In captivity, a great many items may suffice as hides: clay pots, slabs of cork bark, hollow logs, commercially available hide boxes, acrylic logs or artificial tree stumps, and just about anything else that is opaque and large enough for the snake to completely hide inside. Many hobbyists use lengths of PVC pipe. Obtainable at any hardware store, PVC is easily cleaned, is virtually indestructible, and makes an excellent hide for even the largest of corn snakes. Shy individuals, in particular, relish a PVC hide, as one end of the pipe may be nestled under the substrate, with the other end only partially exposed above the substrate. This will give the look and feel of a natural burrow, and a skittish or nervous corn snake will feel much more comfortable when it has something so secure in which to hide.

If deprived of sufficient hiding places, a corn snake will certainly become

Rat snakes will welcome a section of bark to climb on and hide under. An albino black rat snake is shown here.

stressed. Symptoms of insufficient hides includes restlessness, quick, jerky movements, constant roaming about the tank, and excessive nose rubbing. In severe cases, an individual may refuse to feed. Corn snakes, like most snakes, value their security above all else and would sooner starve to death than eat under unsuitable conditions. Situate a variety of hides around the terrarium to ensure that your corn snake has sufficient hiding places.

Security

Not only must the corn snake have a secure feeling inside the terrarium, but the keeper must have a secure enclosure in order to keep the corn snake inside its terrarium. Corn snakes are consummate escape artists and can wriggle, twist, turn, or outright force their way through even the smallest of gaps in the lid of your terrarium. Loose-fitting lids or those that do not lock are common sources of corn snake escapes. Make sure there are no holes, gaps, or cracks in the lid, and that your lid fits snugly and securely on the terrarium itself. Corn snakes are surprisingly strong animals that can force open the corner of a loose-fitting lid or burst right through fine-gauge screen or mesh lids. Keep these escape tendencies in mind while purchasing your terrarium, and do not settle for one with a loose-fitting lid.

A final aspect of terrarium security is to ensure that unwanted intruders don't get in. The household cat, for example, might well have an appetite for a juvenile corn snake, or your neighbor's curious seven-year-old son might not be able to resist tampering with your snake while no one is looking. Locking lids with thick, heavy-gauge screen are perhaps the best solution.

Locks, not Weights

Unfortunately, it is fairly common for hobbyists to use a heavy object or objects, such as books or trophies, to weigh down the lid of their snake enclosure. This is a bad idea for two reasons. One is that it is very easy to forget to put the weights back on or to leave them off "just for a second" as you are feeding or scooping out substrate. The second reason is that as snakes grow, they get stronger. Two heavy dictionaries may have kept your hatchling corn snake or rat snake from getting out for three years, but that is no guarantee it can't get out now. Save yourself the heartache of a lost pet and buy a lid that you can lock.

If the enclosure is not secure, your corn snake will quickly escape, and you will be very lucky if you find it.

Lighting

Many tropical species of snakes and lizards have specific and elaborate needs when it comes to lighting. Fortunately, rat snakes are not among them and have very simple lighting requirements. Corn snakes metabolize their food and vitamins without the aid of ultraviolet (UV) lighting and do not absolutely require special UV bulbs in captivity. However, the psychological benefits of exposure to a UV bulb cannot be denied. Providing your corn snake with at least three to four hours of UV lighting each day makes a big difference in the animal's overall behavior and state of mental wellness. These bulbs come in the form of both incandescent and florescent fixtures. UV lights can be dangerous, however, if you purchase the wrong type. Make sure you only use those varieties sold specifically for reptiles. Avoid tanning bulbs, black lights, and all other nonreptile-specific fixtures.

Standard incandescent light bulbs will illuminate the terrarium while at the same time producing a considerable amount of heat. By placing an incandescent fixture over one end of the tank, you can give your snake a basking spot, which it may or may not utilize. Basking is largely determined by the disposition of the animal in question. There are corn snakes that simply love to bask and those that seek the cover of their hides the minute the lights are turned on.

Florescent fixtures (non-UV), on the other hand, provide a wide range of light but do not produce nearly as much heat as does an incandescent bulb.. Florescent fixtures may also be left turned on all day, and they consume far less power, last longer, and grant a softer, gentler, more even light to the terrarium. Even those skittish corn snakes that hide from incandescent lighting seldom retreat from the florescent lights. I recommend florescent lights for terrariums in which the corn snake is a "show animal," such as in pet shops, doctor's offices, or anywhere else that the tank will be illuminated for long periods each day.

Temperature

Corn snakes, like all snakes, are ectothermic, meaning that they regulate their bodily temperature based on their surrounding environment. If it is warm outside, a corn snake will be warm, but if it's cold out, a corn snake has no choice but to be cold. In the terrarium, a corn snake must be kept warm if it is to live, thrive, grow, and function properly. This heat may come in many forms, and it must be carefully regulated.

No matter how you choose to heat your corn snake's terrarium, you must always supply the animal with both a warm spot in the tank and a cooler spot. A tank that is inescapably hot can kill a corn snake in a matter of minutes, just as an evenly cold tank will cause the snake to languish and wither away over time.

In the wild, a corn snake regulates its body temperature by traveling from areas of greater heat to lesser heat and vice versa. If the snake is too cool, it may slither onto a toasty rock sitting in the sun. When it gets too warm, the snake will seek out a cool, shady retreat where it can cool down. This process is known as behavioral thermoregulation, and a captive corn snake must be able to thermoregulate if it is to thrive under your care. Remember to heat only half of the tank, leaving the other half cooler and shadier, and your corn snake will thermoregulate as it sees fit.

During the periods of the year in which your corn snake is active, the warmest part of its terrarium should be roughly 82° to 84° F (27.8 to 28.9°C), while the cool end should be 72° to 75°F (22.2 to

Because they lack protective skin pigments, snow corns should not be exposed to ultraviolet light.

23.9°C). If you notice your animal spending all its time in the heated end of the terrarium, you might want to consider raising the ambient temperature inside the terrarium by two or three degrees. Placing two thermometers—one at the basking end and one at the cooler end—in the terrarium will help you to regulate the exact temperatures within your corn snake's habitat.

Heating Methods

Using basking lights or heating lamps is a good way to heat part of the terrarium, as well as to provide light for viewing your corn snake. Placing a bulb over one end of the terrarium will create an excellent basking spot. The wattage of bulb you will need will depend on the size of the terrarium. Incandescent bulbs provide the warmest, brightest light, and therefore make the best choice for a basking lamp.

A second type of basking "lamp" is the ceramic heat emitter. Heat emitters are made of thick ceramic molded around a heating coil in the shape of a light bulb, and they screw into incandescent sockets. Because they generate so much heat, heat emitters are only applicable in large terrariums. While they cast no light, ceramic heat emitters generate too much heat to be used near small terrariums. I recommend these items only for the more advanced hobbyist who is already skilled in using heating apparatus. A ceramic heat emitter in the hands of a beginner or child is simply too risky to the captive corn snake.

Undertank heating pads are excellent heating sources. These thin pads adhere to the outside bottom of the terrarium, so there are no cords running under the lid. Heating pads consist of insulated rubber pads in which a series of heating coils are contained. These pads provide even, gentle warmth that soaks up through the bottom of the terrarium. By placing one or two undertank heating pads toward one end of the terrarium, you can provide a safe, stable heated area upon which your corn snake can warm itself at any time, day or night. If your corn snake is shy and doesn't want to bask under a bright light, an undertank heating pad can be the perfect solution, as it provides warmth without any bright lights.

Humidity and Ventilation

Humidity is another very important factor in corn snake husbandry. Too little humidity can cause curling scales, shedding problems, and dehydration. Conversely, too much humidity can

Light and Albinism

Genetically manipulated corn snakes that lack sufficient pigmentation (known as albinos) must never be exposed to UV radiation. They lack melanin in their skins that would protect them from the dangerous effects of ultraviolet light.

Your hatchling corn snake will thrive if kept at temperatures between 72° and 84°F.

lead to skin infections, mold growth, and serious respiratory problems, so balance is the key where humidity is concerned. Purchase a humidity gauge, and place it low on the inside glass of the tank. A good level of relative humidity (what a corn snake would naturally experience in the wild) should be between 60 and 70 percent. Anything above 70 percent will soon become problematic, as will anything below 55 percent. The good news is that unless you live in a swamp or in the desert, the relative humidity of the atmosphere should suffice for your corn snake to thrive. The only other variables that could affect the level of humidity inside the terrarium are the substrate you use, the amount of liquid in the terrarium (the size of the water bowl), and the degree of ventilation the terrarium receives.

Substrates such as newspapers, sand, and dry bark chips will actually lower the humidity in a terrarium and may cause the skin and scales of your snake to dry out, curl, or crack. Substrates such as peat moss or mulch may hold excessive moisture and can lead to higher levels of humidity. The key to balancing humidity is to have a well-ventilated terrarium. Ventilation is simply the amount of air that passes through the terrarium, and it can typically be optimized by covering the terrarium with a screen lid, which allows not only for fresh oxygen to enter the tank, but also for moisture and foul odors to disperse. Especially in the case of elaborate, living vivaria, which contain an enormous amount of organic material, live

Don't Use Hot Rocks

Heating rocks, or "hot rocks," were once used by hobbyists far and wide, but they are now seen as less than perfect as a means for providing heat to reptiles. Not only do their electric cords have to run into the terrarium from the wall socket (thereby leaving a gap at the lid through which your corn snake might escape), but hot rocks are oftentimes faulty in their wiring and construction. Made of a polymer compound molded around a coil of wire, a hot rock's polymer may be thin in some areas, causing hot spots to occur on the stone. These spots may reach very high temperatures and can seriously burn your corn snake. Very small corn snakes may try to burrow under the edge of a hot rock, get stuck there, and die in a very short amount of time. Aside from their being unsafe, hot rocks are also quite inefficient; the rock only warms the area immediately surrounding it and leaves the rest of the terrarium totally unheated. For these reasons and more, I strongly advise against using hot rocks in the corn snake terrarium.

plants, and permanent water sources, noxious gases such as ammonia can build up in the lower depths of the terrarium, thereby causing harm to your corn snake. Supplementing such a terrarium with a ventilation fan is a good idea, as the fan's movement will disperse the noxious gases and stimulate healthy oxygen flow.

If your corn snake is spending a lot of time in its water bowl, the enclosure could be too dry or too hot.

If you find that your terrarium is too dry, and your corn snake is suffering from curling scales or dehydration, you might want to add another dish of water to the terrarium, which will increase humidity as the water evaporates. Turning off any ventilation fans and covering one-third of the lid with cellophane will help to trap escaping moisture and raise humidity levels in the terrarium. Fortunately, corn snakes naturally occur in fairly humid environments, so they can tolerate a wide range of humidity.

Chapter 3

Choosing Your Corn Snake

Easily the most important moment of any corn snake endeavor is the initial purchase. If you pick out a healthy animal, then all other aspects of husbandry, care, and breeding should fall into place nicely and with minimal problems. If, however, you purchase a weak, sickly, or otherwise "sub-par" corn snake, you may well be starting off down a long and wearisome road, as unhealthy animals may be predisposed to any number of problems and complications in captivity. Fortunately, it is fairly easy to avoid purchasing a "problem snake." Corn snakes are, by nature, very hardy, disease resistant, and accommodating as pets. By following a few simple rules and guidelines, you'll soon develop a discriminating eye for only the finest corn snakes available.

Picking a Healthy Snake
The Snake Itself

The term *healthy* is a deceptively simple word that encompasses a wide range of considerations. The first is behavior, which will vary based on the age and disposition of the specimen in question. In nature, corn snakes are shy animals and are quick to hide themselves from would-be predators. In the case of hatchling or juvenile corn snakes, all healthy animals should display this cryptic behavior. As you approach the tank in the pet shop, the baby corn snakes should be hiding inside or under some type of hide. If not in hiding, the snakes should be slithering, climbing, crawling, or doing something else that looks like a normal, active behavior. Baby corn snakes that are lying completely stretched out, not moving, or acting "funny" (i.e., moving in short, jerky motions) should be avoided, as such behaviors are not natural.

A healthy corn snake will have clear eyes and no crust or discharge around the nostrils.

If the animal you are considering purchasing is not a juvenile, however, it may well be accustomed to the presence of human beings, and all the rules change. Your tame dog doesn't run and hide when it sees you, and a tame corn snake won't either. Tame corn snakes often lay fully exposed in their terrarium. They have come to accept the handling by humans and are comfortable in their surroundings; thus, they may not hide at your approach.

There is a second aspect of behavior. Once you have found a corn snake that acts normally, you'll want to handle it to determine its disposition. Young or hatchling corn snakes are often quite defensive (after all, you are a lot bigger than they are!) at your approach. They may coil and strike repeatedly. That's okay. They are not yet used to human presence. Striking behavior, incidentally, is also a sign of good health. It tells you that the young snake is strong, alert, and keenly aware of what is going on in the world around it.

Once you pick up a baby corn snake, it should become apparent what its disposition is. Does it strike? Does it slither calmly about your fingers? Does it lay limp and motionless in your hands? Limp and motionless animals must be avoided, as motionlessness may be associated with skeletal, nerve, or muscular deformities. Whatever it does when you pick it up, a healthy baby corn snake will do something active: It will move, flick its tongue, slither, strike, try to escape, or even empty its cloacal contents on you!

Again, the rules change slightly if the animal in question is an adult. Hatchling or juvenile corn snakes that strike savagely can be tamed in time, but adult specimens that have been in captivity for a while and still display such aggressive behavior will not likely become tame any time soon and should not be purchased. Fortunately, these animals are extremely rare and are often the result of eggs that incubated at very high temperatures. Even wild-caught adult corn snakes typically tame quickly, so an aggressive adult is likely to have some neurological problem that will never allow the animal to become tame.

Check for Mites

There is an easy test you can conduct to check for mites and external parasites adhering to the skin of a snake you may want to buy. Wet a white paper towel, lay it in the palm of your hand, close this hand around the corn snake, and allow the animal to slither completely through your hand. Look at the paper towel. Is it still clean, or does it have tiny specks crawling around on it? These specks are mites, and they can present serious problems in the corn snake terrarium. Do not purchase any snake—regardless of its beauty—that suffers from mites.

Only purchase a corn snake that is appropriately housed in a clean enclosure.

Now that you have the corn snake—be it a juvenile or adult—in your hands, it's time to inspect it physically. Does it have any cuts, scrapes, or lesions? Are there any lumps under the skin? How does its belly look? Is its belly smooth and evenly textured, or are there spots of cankered flesh and discoloration? A healthy corn snake will have smooth, even scales that are not curled, cankered, nor discolored. The belly of starved or underfed individuals will be sunken or concave. Healthy snakes, even babies, will have a flat, firm belly, and they should have a noticeable body weight—the snake should feel as heavy as it looks. Avoid purchasing any animals that have cuts, lesions, sores, curling scales, or concave/gaunt features. Rat snakes are powerful, muscular creatures, and you should be able to feel the muscles—rigid and strong—moving under the skin when you touch one. The backbone and ribs of a healthy animal should not protrude at all.

Next, look at the animal's head. The eyes should be clean and free of any debris or parasites, and the nose should be free from any crust or exudate. Does the mouth close all the way, or does it appear to be packed with brown or cheesy gunk? How frequently does the tongue flicker? Does the head turn to look at you, or does it hang limp? Any obstruction around the eyes, nose, or mouth is a warning sign that something is definitely wrong with that animal, and you should look for another corn snake.

The Snake's Surroundings

Another rule of thumb when purchasing a corn snake is to inspect the animal's surroundings. Does the shopkeeper house the snake in a clean, well-kept terrarium, or has he or she crammed two dozen baby corns into a filthy 10-gallon (38 l) tank? Even if you find a corn snake that passes all of the aforementioned considerations, if it has spent any length of time housed under such disgustingly filthy conditions, chances are it may be in the early stages of some internal ailment or another and will likely fall ill soon after you get it home.

A Test

A final, critical aspect of a healthy corn snake will be determined when the individual in question is offered a meal. Always ask to see an animal eat before making a purchase, as a perfectly healthy corn snake that refuses to feed will not stay perfectly healthy for long. The exception to this would be if the corn snake is about to shed and has cloudy eyes. No self-respecting pet shop owner will refuse you this request, and if he or she does, I'd start looking for my corn snake elsewhere. A healthy corn snake will attack its food with much gusto: striking, coiling, and constricting even a pre-killed prey item as

Hold the Sympathy

It may be highly tempting to buy an obviously sick corn snake in hopes of saving it, but don't do it. Purchasing a sick corn snake in order to rehabilitate it almost always ends with the snake dead, your bank account smaller, and your heart broken. It is very difficult to rehabilitate a sick snake, even for veterinarians and wildlife rehabilitators. Additionally, by purchasing a sick corn snake, you have financially rewarded a vendor for mistreating his or her animals. It is better to pass on the snake (that will most likely die whether you buy it or not), inform the vendor that the snake is sick, and take your business elsewhere.

though it were alive. The corn snake will swallow its meal quickly and may roam about the tank for a few minutes searching for more prey. After the corn snake has fed, you'll want to give it at least 48 hours to fully digest its meal before making the purchase and transporting the animal home. Transporting a corn snake before it has digested its meal could result in severe stress and regurgitation—a nasty way to begin your corn snake endeavor!

Quarantining

An important, and often overlooked, aspect of corn snake and rat snake husbandry is the

It is a good idea to observe a snake feed before purchasing it. Obviously, this Texas rat snake has a good appetite.

quarantine period. Because a great many reptilian diseases are highly communicable, bringing an infected individual into close contact with the rest of your herp collection can lead to devastating results. Select a room in your house that is well away from the rest of your reptiles, and place your quarantine tank there. Depending on the size of your new acquisition, the tank may need to be larger or smaller. I have found a 20-gallon (76 l) "long" tank provides adequate room for corn snakes of just about any size. Outfit the quarantine tank with a white paper towel substrate, a small dish of clean water, and a plastic or other artificial hide. The conditions of the tank should be very sparse, clean, and hospital-like. Illuminate, heat, and feed the corn snake as you normally would for about a month, but do not remove it from quarantine.

During these weeks, it is your duty to watch the new corn snake closely. Does it move or act "funny?" Do you see tiny parasites (mites) crawling on the paper towels or drowning in the water dish? Does the snake hold its mouth agape constantly or seem to have problems breathing? Does it vomit or have intensely sweet- or foul-smelling stool? Does the corn snake

Most captive-bred corn and rat snakes sold to hobbyists are healthy, but quarantine is still a recommended precaution. A creamsickle corn snake is pictured.

produce excess mucus from its nose or mouth? All of these are warning signs that something is seriously wrong with your new corn snake and will become evident while the snake is in quarantine. If any of these signs manifest, you should seek veterinary care immediately. If the corn snake is healthy and free of parasites, its month in quarantine will pass uneventfully, and that animal can safely be brought into your herp collection. Even if you have no other herps, quarantine is still an excellent idea, as this period of close observation will prevent any ailments or parasites from passing undetected and allow you to provide veterinary care as soon as possible.

Not only is a quarantine tank good for the initial observation period, it is also an excellent place where sickly or injured corn snakes can make a recovery. Warm, sterile conditions will go a long way toward putting your ailing corn snake back on the road to recovery.

Chapter 4

Caring for Your Corn Snake

One of the most desirable aspects of the corn snake is the ease of care in captivity. These snakes are extremely hardy, and they can thrive under the hand of even the most novice hobbyist. While corn snakes, unlike boas and pythons, are very undemanding, they still must receive certain care if they are to not just survive, but thrive.

Feeding

In over two decades of keeping and breeding corn snakes, I can't remember a single one of my animals that refused to feed in captivity. Corn snakes naturally have excellent appetites, and they aren't shy about showing it. In fact, the hobbyist may have to be careful that his or her fingers don't come between a hungry corn snake and its meal, as an overly enthusiastic corn snake might accidentally bite the hand that feeds it.

Using feeding tongs is often a great solution to this problem. Grasp the prekilled prey item by the tail (or wing/foot) with the tongs, insert the tongs into the terrarium, and jiggle the rodent around. When the hungry corn snake is enticed into striking, your fingers will be safely on the outside of the terrarium. Some corn snakes can be particular about when they eat and may never accept meals during the day or when the lights are on. In the case of these animals, it's best to simply place the prekilled food item in the terrarium just before turning out the lights. You can check on the prey in a few hours with the aid of a flashlight and see if it has been consumed. If not eaten within six to eight hours, dispose of the prekilled rodent and try again in a few days with a fresh rodent. Allowing your corn snake to consume rotting prey is a great way to make it very sick!

The occasional corn snake may be a bit shy about taking a meal while you are watching. These secretive snakes are often coaxed into taking food if it is jiggled directly in front of the snake's hiding box. If your corn snake is having problems eating, just try leaving the rodent at the door of the hide. You might be surprised at how quickly the corn snake strikes the prey and drags it into the hide to be consumed.

While it is common knowledge that all species of snakes can consume meals that are larger than their heads, this elasticity has its limits. Never feed your corn snake any prey item that is larger than 1.5 times the diameter of its neck. Corn snakes are such ravenous predators that if presented with very large prey, they will likely try to devour it anyway. A continual

Hatchling corn snakes and rat snakes (gray rat snake pictured) are normally fed hairless baby mice, called pinkies.

Just in Case

If your corn snake ever does bite you, don't pull away, as you'll likely tear your flesh, making a nasty wound from a minor injury and possibly breaking the snake's teeth. Once the corn snake figures out you aren't its dinner, it will let go. Wash the wound with warm, soapy water, apply a topical antiseptic cream, and watch for infection. Remember that even a large adult corn snake is unlikely to cause a serious injury. Just keep your hands clear of the tank when feeding time rolls around, and you should be fine.

diet of very large prey items can severely damage the nerves, skin, and esophagus of your corn snake. Feeding a larger number of smaller meals to your corn snake is definitely safer and healthier than feeding fewer, larger meals.

Captive Diet

In the wild, corn snakes feed on just about anything that is warm-blooded and small enough to fit in their mouths: field mice, rats, chipmunks, moles, birds, bird eggs, bats, baby squirrels, baby rabbits, and more. While replicating such dietary variety in captivity is all but impossible, it is still important that we offer our corn snakes as wide a variety of fare as possible, as some prey items provide more nutrients than do others.

Rodents Small, commercially raised mice are the typical food staple of captive corns and are readily available from pet shops and online retailers specializing in live feeders. Frozen feeder mice may also be purchased. Shipped overnight and packed on dry ice, these "mouse-cicles" may be kept in the freezer until your corn snake is ready to eat them. Simply thaw the mouse for at least four hours in a tub of warm water, dry it off, and offer it to your corn snake. Most hobbyists agree that frozen mice are much easier and more convenient than live feeders, and if bought in lots of 25, 50, or more, are also far less expensive per mouse.

Of course, commercially raised mice are not the most nutritious of foods. Wild mice, rats, and other rodents, because they consume such a wide variety of nuts, grains, and vegetables, are highly nutritious and will be welcomed by your corn snake. However, the drawback to feeding wild rodents is that those rodents may have been subjected to poisons, pesticides, or other agricultural impurities that could harm your corn snake. Likewise, wild rodents may be infected with bacteria, internal parasites, or some other disease that could infect your corn snake.

Corn snakes will not hesitate to prey on birds, in this case a summer tanager. You can offer your snake farm-raised chicks, if you desire.

Chickens Chicks and chicken eggs are also highly nutritious, but they should only be offered as treats, not as a staple. Feeding one newly hatched chick every two weeks will improve your corn snake's scales, sheen, and promote healthy shed cycles, as the protein in the chick or eggs does wonders for growth and scale development. Chicks (or quail chicks) are not as readily available as are mice, but if you can find some at a reasonable price, I highly recommend feeding them on occasion.

Other Options Some hobbyists feed chunks of chicken, beef, or pork to their corn snakes, and think they are saving a few bucks by doing so. While beef hunks are cheaper than frozen mice, they are also grossly unhealthy for your corn snake, and a diet of such muscle meats can lead to kidney and liver failure, obesity, and a host of other metabolic maladies in your pet. Likewise, cut hunks of meat do not supply the calcium (found in bone) that your corn snake would receive from a white mouse or chick. Never feed your corn snake anything other than whole organisms.

Another food option is the so-called "snake sausages." Made from ground-up chicks and mice,

Hands Off!
Refrain from handling your corn snake for at least 48 hours after feeding. Handling or other undue stress can cause the corn snake to regurgitate its semi-digested meal.

these meaty links are packed into skins, just like real sausages, and can be fed to corn snakes of any age. Like chicks or chicken eggs, however, these items should be offered only as treats and never as a staple diet. Corn snakes that feed exclusively on snake sausages or other such manufactured foods often suffer from obesity, malnutrition, and vitamin/mineral deficiency. I recommend feeding such items no more frequently than once every month.

As your corn snake grows, you must offer it correspondingly larger prey.

Live Food or Prekilled?

When it comes to feeding corn snakes, hobbyists typically subscribe to one of two schools of thought. Members of the first camp hold the notion that food offered live is best. Corn snakes and rat snakes are masterful predators that have, for the past 50 million years, been catching, subduing, and consuming live prey items. Members of the opposing camp adhere to the philosophy that prekilled prey items are much safer to offer to our pets. Many wild corn snakes bear scars, missing eyes, and misshapen snouts, possibly from the last-ditch efforts of their prey. Feeding prekilled prey eliminates the chance your snake will be injured by its food. By virtue of your corn snake never having to exercise its hunting and killing instincts in captivity, some hobbyists argue that your snake remains docile; the snake is not likely to mistake the hand that feeds it for a moving prey item.

Some hobbyists even argue for prekilled prey items from a humane standpoint. Prekilling a mouse alleviates much of the trauma and panic that death by snake constriction entails.

Whether you feed prekilled or live is largely a matter of choice and preference. Corn snakes will readily accept prekilled mice, and they should have no problem in subduing and constricting any live prey items to death (but accidents do happen). If you do feed live prey items, bear in mind that a mouse or a rat is a living animal with a strong will to live and *very* sharp teeth. Leaving a rat in your corn snake's cage is highly irresponsible and dangerous to the snake, as an unchecked rat can seriously bite and injure your pet snake.

Feeding Schedule

A common problem in corn snake husbandry is improper feeding. Some hobbyists feed too infrequently. Conversely, some hobbyists feed their pets far too frequently, resulting in a gigantic, malformed snake that is highly prone to serious health problems. Known as "power feeding," this practice of overfeeding is often purposeful, as the hobbyist wishes to raise an enormous corn snake or get one to breeding size as quickly as possible. Be warned, however, that power feeding is a heinous practice; while the musculature of the corn snake will grow rapidly, the skeletal, neurological, and organ systems will not develop properly. The result is an unhealthy corn snake that will not likely live longer than eight to ten years and that will likely die of organ failure sooner than that.

In order to avoid over- or underfeeding your corn snake, a feeding schedule is advisable. By adhering to a schedule similar to the one in the table below, you can keep a firm grasp on just how much your corn snake is eating and how fast it should grow and still stay at peak health. Hatchling corn snakes require more food, as they are naturally developing at the most rapid rate of their lives. As they get a little older, they will grow more slowly, but they still

Corn and Rat Snake Feeding Schedule

Age of Snake	Size of Meal	Frequency of Meals
Hatchling-6 months	Pinkie mice	1 every 3-4 days
6 months-1 years	Pinkie/fuzzy mice	1 every 3-4 days
1 years-2 years	Adult mice	1 every 4-5 days
2 years-3 years	Adult mice	1-2 every 5-6 days
3 years +	Small rats, chicks, adult mice	1-2 every 6-7 days

Most snakes are overfed in captivity. Monitor your corn snake's weight to prevent it from becoming obese.

need considerable amounts of food as they near sexual maturity. Older adult specimens grow the slowest of all but can be fed on a regular basis without much fear of overfeeding. Very large adult corn snakes may take larger meals, and hobbyists will have to gauge for themselves just how much to feed.

The only exceptions to this schedule come in the form of ailing or prebreeding corn snakes. Sick or underweight animals may require more frequent feedings until they can recover and attain an acceptable body weight. Once such an animal is well again, its feeding should resume as per your schedule. Likewise, females that will soon be bred should be offered larger amounts of food, as they will certainly need the extra nutrients and energy to produce a large, healthy clutch of eggs.

Vitamins & Minerals

Captive corn snakes do not receive all the necessary vitamins and minerals that they would get in nature. This is simply due to the limited variety of food items we as hobbyists can offer. As a result, we must supplement our pets' diets with extra vitamins and minerals. Available at pet shops and online, herpetological vitamins and minerals come in the forms of powders and liquids and can be either dusted into the fur or feathers of the corn snake's next meal or injected (in liquid form) into the prekilled prey item.

Caring for Your Corn Snake   43

Because they are experiencing a rapid period of growth, hatchling and juvenile corn snakes require more vitamin and mineral supplements than do older corn snakes. Dust each meal with a calcium/phosphorous supplement, the ratio being 3:1. Calcium is very important for proper bone development and skeletal growth, but it is useless without the proper amount of vitamin D3. D3 is necessary for a reptile's ability to metabolize calcium. Without D3, all reptiles would simply pass the calcium right out of their systems and would never benefit from it. Most reptile-specific calcium supplements come mixed with the proper amounts of vitamin D3.

When adding vitamin supplements, the hobbyist must take care not to overdose his or her corn snake. Some vitamins, such as vitamin A, can accumulate in your animal's system and can quickly become toxic. Hatchlings and juvenile corn snakes are especially susceptible to vitamin toxicity and should be offered a vitamin supplement no more frequently than once every third feeding. Dust the prey item in the same way that you do with the calcium supplement.

Not all authorities agree that snakes need to have their diets supplemented. The reasoning is that the snake is eating a whole prey item that is in and of itself nutritionally complete. The snake digests the bones, brains, skin, and internal organs, thus receiving complete nutrition. This is a topic that continues to divide keepers. Consult your reptile veterinarian if you are in doubt about whether you should supplement or not.

Snakes will be noticeably swollen after a meal, as this Baird's rat snake is.

Obesity

Obesity most often occurs in corn snakes that have been fed too much and exercised too infrequently. Symptoms of obesity include sluggishness, lethargy, the inability to coil tightly, and skin showing in between the scales. They may display tiny rolls of excess fat along their sides as they coil. Obese corn snakes must be offered food less frequently, and they should be taken out of their terrariums and exercised (allowed to slither about, climb, swim, and generally remain active) for at least an hour each day. Once its feeding schedule has been amended and it exercises daily, an obese corn snake should begin to trim down in a matter of weeks. Allowing your corn snake to remain obese will expose it to the same health risks that threaten humans: high blood pressure, heart troubles, and generally shortened life span.

Water

Watering your corn snake is very easy. Simply leave a dish of clean, fresh water at your corn snake's disposal at all times. To avoid contamination or illness, you must change the water daily. Every day, remove the water dish, wash it in hot, soapy water, rinse thoroughly, and replace with fresh water. If left sitting too long, the water will stagnate, and cultures of bacteria and other microorganisms will begin growing in the dish. If ingested by your corn snake, some of these bacteria can cause dysentery or other illnesses. For all the same reasons that we as humans do not drink stagnant, soured water, our corn snakes shouldn't have to, either.

In rare cases, your corn snake might crawl into its water dish and stay there for a prolonged period of time. Either the animal is having trouble shedding its skin and needs to soak in order to loosen and shed its old skin, or it may be suffering from external parasites. Corn snakes having open sores or lesions may crawl into their water dish to find relief from the pain of their wounds. In either case, the snake should not be allowed to spend excessive amounts of time in its water dish, as continual exposure to moisture will quickly lead to a serious skin problem known as blister disease. Remedy the problem by first making sure your snake is not suffering from retained skin, parasites, or skin ailments. Then, if one of these problems is not the cause, replace the water dish with a much smaller one into which the corn snake cannot fit.

Extra precautions must be taken when providing a water dish to hatchling or juvenile specimens. Use very shallow dishes with gradually sloping sides, as deep water dishes with steep sides can easily prove to be a death trap to a young corn snake.

Exercise & Handling

Daily or bi-daily periods of "exercise" will help to maintain a healthy appetite and attitude in your corn snake. Corn snakes are some of the most intelligent of all colubrids, and they have definite dispositions and attitudes. They need mental stimulation much like a pet bird or dog. Corn snakes that are never taken out and played with can become sluggish, slow, and possibly hostile, as their mental and physical malaise only worsens when they are continually subjected to a nonstimulating environment. Conversely, the corn snake that is often touched, handled, and exercised is swift, keen, and often comes right up to the glass of its terrarium whenever the keeper enters the room. Corn snakes seem to enjoy the movement, stimulation, and warmth of their keepers. They need to flex their muscles and explore the sights and smells of their surroundings, and if they are to thrive under your care, they must not be denied such activities in captivity. Exercise in this instance means handling the snake and keeping it on the move. You can also let your corn snake roam a bit, but only under close supervision. Do not let your snake slither under furniture or near heating ducts, drains, or the like.

Regular exercise also promotes muscular development, proper skeletal and tendon development (which is particularly important in hatchling and juvenile specimens), regular bowel movements, and minimizes the risk of obesity. Animals that are thoroughly and regularly handled and exercised by their keepers live longer, on average, than those animals kept shut away in their terrariums.

Keep your corn snake's water bowl clean at all times. A striped albino corn snake is pictured.

Female corn snakes that are breeding stock also produce larger, typically healthier clutches of eggs and recover more quickly from egg deposition if they have been regularly handled and exercised throughout their lives. All in all, regular handling reduces stress, promotes health, and greatly increases the quality of life in all corn snakes.

Aside from all those health aspects, handling your corn snake is downright fun! Handling gives hobbyists the chance to get as close as possible to our serpentine pets. Handling is the difference between our corn snakes as animals and our corn snakes as friends. There are so many reptile species on the market that would bite, lash, claw, or slash you sooner than let you pick them up, so we should enjoy the benevolence of our chosen pets every chance we get. Because corn snakes are so easily handled, we should pick them up and play with them daily. Both you and your corn snake will be better off for it!

Handling Do's and Dont's

When handling your corn snake, there are certain rules or practices that are important. If handling a baby or juvenile corn snake, be careful not to suddenly grasp or squeeze it, as its skeleton and muscles are still delicate, and a firm grasp by a human hand can cause serious internal injury. Let a baby corn snake slither as it likes, while you support its body in your hands. When picking it up from the terrarium, let it slither into your hands, perhaps by gentle coaxing, but certainly do not grasp it as you would an adult snake.

Once the corn snake is a little older and firmer of body, it is safe to pick it up, hold it, and generally handle it a little more casually than you would a fragile hatchling. Corn snakes, as a general rule, should be allowed to roam as they like, the active part of handling being done by the snake, not by the keeper.

Corn snakes also have two sensitive areas where they *really* don't like to be touched: the head and the tail. The head, and about 6 inches (15.2cm) down the neck, of the corn snake is a sensitive area. Corn snakes like this portion of their body to be able to move uninhibited, and despite their normally benign disposition, they can get irritated quickly if their head is molested or restrained. Likewise, the tail is a sensitive region, and a corn snake will pull away quickly if its tail is grasped, pinched, or otherwise tampered with, as this is the region where

The Water Bowl as Swimming Pool

One other reason corn and other rat snakes may sit in their water bowls is to deal with high temperatures. If your snake is too hot, it will try to cool itself any way it can. This may mean soaking in the water bowl if the cool end of the cage is too warm. If your corn snake is spending all its time in the water bowl, be sure to check the cage temperatures and adjust them if necessary.

the genitals and cloaca are located. It makes sense if you think about it. If some stranger made a sudden and uninvited grasp at your face or genitals, you'd likely pull away very quickly, too!

Hygiene

There are downsides to all that handling, but with a little common sense, these never have to become problematic. No matter how much affection we may shower upon our corn snakes, we must bear in mind that these animals live in a terrarium, do not bathe, and never wash themselves off

Always wash your hands before and after handling pet snakes.

with antibacterial hand soap. The nooks and crannies of their scales can and do pick up minute bits of debris, feces, and other media in which bacteria can grow. Healthy animals and those maintained in the most hygienic conditions are less likely to carry bacteria on their bodies, but all are capable of spreading infection.

The worst of these bacteria is *Salmonella*, which can cause serious, painful, and long-lasting symptoms in a human host. In the late 1980s and early 1990s, large numbers of people expressed growing concern regarding the *Salmonella* epidemic as it related to reptiles. Scores of children were hospitalized with infections, and many contracted it from their reptilian pets. (Of course, it didn't come to light until much later that the lion's share of the infected persons housed their animals in filthy enclosures, and many were young children who put the animals in their mouths.) While this situation is a real concern, there are certain rules of sanitation that can prevent such contamination:

- Maintain a clean terrarium and facilities. As soon as your animal defecates, clean the tank thoroughly.
- Always wash your hands thoroughly with an antibacterial soap immediately before and after handling your corn snake.
- Never put any part of the snake in your mouth. Do not let it come close to your face, eyes, or nose.

- Never put your hands in your mouth while handling your corn snake.
- If your corn snake crawls through its own waste, give it a bath in clean, lukewarm water (no soap), and change its substrate immediately.

These few, simple rules will make all the difference in the hygiene of your corn snake. Think about it this way: You wouldn't break eggs in a bowl, leave them sitting out overnight, and scramble and eat them the next morning, right? That would be ridiculously unsafe. The same holds true for corn snake sanitation. Just use a little common sense, and you'll have no problems.

The flip side of safe sanitation is for the benefit of the corn snake itself. As we go about our daily lives, we may put any number of chemical agents on our bodies: soaps, dyes, colognes, perfumes, lotions, creams, cleaners, etc. While we may not experience any ill effects from these agents, our corn snakes could be at a terrible risk. Exposure to most household chemicals can cause skin, eye, olfactory, or respiratory damage to your corn snake. Extreme cases of chemical exposure can result in death.

By the same token, handling one sick or infected animal in your herp collection, not washing your hands, and then handling your corn snake is an almost guaranteed way to spread disease or contamination to an otherwise perfectly healthy corn snake. It is, therefore, critically important that we as hobbyists decontaminate ourselves thoroughly before picking up or handling our corn snakes. The best way of doing this is simply to wash our hands with hot water, antibacterial soap, and rinse thoroughly in clean water. Doing so will go a long way toward ensuring the continued health of our beloved pets.

Keeping your corn snake's cage clean will go a long way toward keeping it—and yourself—healthy. A caramel corn is pictured.

Chapter 5

Health Care

While corn snakes are highly resistant to ailments and diseases, they are certainly not immune to them. In fact, there are several ailments that afflict corn snakes all too often. Fortunately, following sound rules of husbandry and sanitation can prevent most of these diseases, and most, if caught early, are easily treated and cured. I would like to stress at this point the necessity of a herp-specific veterinarian. Taking your newly acquired animal(s) to your veterinarian for an initial inspection, as well as returning for an annual physical checkup, is paramount in avoiding any one of these diseases. All the diseases and treatments discussed here are applicable to all species of North American rat snakes.

The Hospital Tank

The same terrarium that you use as a quarantine tank for newly acquired individuals can also be used as a hospital or sick tank for any ailing corn snakes. Outfit a hospital tank much in the same manner as a quarantine tank: white paper towel substrate, a plastic hide box, a small water dish, appropriate heating device, and nothing else. In the hospital tank, the corn snake must be observed closely; therefore, there is no room for lots of climbing branches or décor, which would obscure the animal from view.

The hospital tank should be kept slightly warmer than the standard terrarium. Warmer temperatures, something along the lines of 85° to 87° F (29.4° to 30.6°C), will stimulate your corn snake's immune system and will make a big difference in the rate at which your pet recovers. Monitor the temperature closely to be sure that the cool end is at least 5 degrees cooler than the rest of the tank. Most sick corn snakes will seek out the higher temperatures. Even wild corn snakes, when they are sick, will instinctively seek out warmer areas to heal themselves.

Because many of the ailments that afflict corn snakes are communicable and can pose a threat to any other herps you may own, the hospital tank should be kept far away from your reptile collection, preferably in another room altogether. Change the substrate as soon as is necessary in the hospital tank, as this terrarium must stay clean at all times. Always remember to wash your hands thoroughly in hot, soapy water after handling a sick corn snake.

If you think your corn snake is ill, it is much better to seek treatment from a herp veterinarian sooner rather than later.

Parasites

Parasites are not often encountered on captive-bred corn snakes, but they often afflict wild individuals. If you use wood and furnishings from outdoors without first treating them, your snakes may frequently be plagued by parasites. Additionally, feeding your corn snake wild rodents, birds, or lizards increases the chances your snake will contract a parasitic infection. The best way to avoid parasites of all types is to buy a captive-bred corn snake and prevent your pet from being exposed to wild-caught reptiles.

Finding a Herp Vet

It is not always easy to find vets who are experienced with reptiles and amphibians. Here are some suggestions to help you locate a vet who can help with your pet corn or rat snake. It is best if you locate one before you actually have an emergency.

- Call veterinarians listed as "exotic" or "reptile" vets in the phonebook. Ask them questions to be sure they are familiar with rat snakes.
- Ask at your local pet stores, zoos, and animal shelters to see if there is someone they can recommend.
- Herpetological societies are likely to know which local vets treat reptiles and amphibians.
- Contact the Association of Reptilian and Amphibian Veterinarians. Their website is www.arav.org.

Ticks & Mites

Both ticks and mites are bloodsucking parasites that attach themselves to the skin of your corn snake, and both can present a very serious problem if left to their own devices.

Ticks The less dangerous of the two, ticks usually appear as small (10 mm) crab-looking creatures that usually attach themselves near the eyes, edges of the mouth, and around the cloaca. Ticks are drawn to these areas, as they are poorly scaled and receive lots of blood flow.

Remove ticks by grasping them gently with a pair of tweezers and slowly pulling until the tick releases its grip. Do not pull quickly or jerk the tweezers back, as this sudden motion will likely tear the tick in two—removing its body, but leaving the head and mandibles firmly attached to your corn snake. Retained heads are often the cause of more serious infections. Dabbing a bit of petroleum jelly or mineral oil on a tick about an hour prior to removal will usually make the task much easier, as the suffocated tick may die or release its bite on its own. After removing a tick, swab the attachment site with a topical antibiotic cream, and monitor for infection.

Mites Mites are insidious parasites that reproduce very quickly if left unchecked. Appearing as tiny (about the size of a fleck of pepper) red, brownish, or black dots crawling all over your corn snake, these miniscule parasites are dangerous and must be destroyed quickly and thoroughly to prevent future outbreaks. Steps for combating a mite infestation are as follows:

- Remove the afflicted corn snake from his terrarium.
- Bathe the animal in lukewarm water, massaging the scales and washing away as many mites as possible.
- Place bathed snake in quarantine.
- Dispose of all organic and noncleanable substrate and décor in the infested terrarium. Tie up the garbage bag and take outside immediately.
- Wash all inorganic environs (large rocks, hides, water dishes etc.) in *soapy, scalding-hot water* mixed with about 10 percent bleach. Rinse well.
- Scald the terrarium with the soapy water and bleach, making sure to wash every little crack and corner, as mites will take refuge around the top and at the seams. Rinse well.

Wild corn snakes usually have ticks, mites, and other parasites.

Because mites can lay their eggs virtually anywhere within the terrarium, the scalding of all inorganic materials and the disposal of all organic materials is absolutely necessary, as when the eggs hatch, the infestation will occur again about two weeks after you think you've beaten it.

To treat the snake itself, there are a number of options. You can spray the hospital tank with Provent-A-Mite and then place the snake in the cage. As of this writing, this product appears to be safe to use in all snakes and lizards and is an effective mite killer. Another way to dispose of mites on the snake itself is to give him a bath in a lukewarm solution of water and povidone-iodine (available in drugstores). Make the solution dilute—the solution should be the color of weak tea. Change the water several times, and make sure the snake is completely submerged a few times—obviously, do not drown it.

Internal Parasites

Internal parasites come in a wide variety of types (roundworms, flukes, flatworms, amoebas, coccidia, nematodes, tapeworms, and trichomonads) and often can be impossible to

Mites can seriously erode the health of your snake, especially if it is a hatchling like this Great Plains rat snake.

diagnose without a microscope and a skilled veterinarian. Symptoms of internal parasite infestation include:

- Unexplained and sudden weight loss.
- Intensely sweet- or foul-smelling stool.
- Frequent vomiting.
- Bloody, runny, or mucoid stool.
- Healthy appetite accompanied by continual weight loss.
- Sudden loss of appetite combined with any of the above signs.

Once diagnosed, the internal parasite infestation should be treated only under the direct care of your veterinarian, as an overdose or misapplication of the medicines required to combat the parasites can often prove as dangerous as the infestation itself.

Cryptosporidiosis Perhaps the most dangerous of all internal parasites is *Cryptosporidium*, a dangerous

Pest Strips

Until recently, the standard mite treatment was to use vapona-impregnated insect-killing strips. However, more and more evidence is accumulating that these strips can cause death or injury in herps, sometimes many months after they have been used. It is probably best to avoid using them.

protozoan that colonizes the corn snake's digestive tract and causes vomiting, severe swelling and bloating, and rapid weight loss. An infection with this parasite is called cryptosporidiosis. There is currently no known cure for cryptosporidiosis, and any infected animals

A view of the midbody swelling characteristic of a *Cryptosporidium* infection. There is no cure for this illness, and this poor snow corn was probably euthanized.

should be dispatched as humanely as possible. The *Cryptosporidium* is also highly infectious; it can quickly spread through and devastate an entire herp collection. It's best to dispose of the affected animal as soon as the parasite is detected.

Perhaps the worst aspect of this foul parasite is that it may be present in its host for up to two years before manifesting any signs of infection. An entire snake collection could be infected, and the average hobbyist would never suspect anything until it was too late. The good news is that *Cryptosporidium* is very rare in corn snakes and can largely be guarded against by maintaining clean facilities.

Infections
Mouth Rot

Mouth rot, technically known as infectious stomatitis, is a condition in which the mouth, and eventually the throat and lung, of a corn snake becomes infected by bacteria and possibly fungi. Brought about by unsanitary living conditions and excessively low temperatures, mouth rot is extremely painful to the corn snake, and, in severe cases, may cause serious jaw and facial disfigurement. If left untreated, mouth rot is fatal.

Symptoms include the formation of a cheesy, whitish to yellow exudate in the mouth, the blackening and/or falling out of the teeth, reddened and inflamed gums, refusal to feed, and a frequent opening of the mouth. Inspect your corn snake's mouth by grasping the animal gently but firmly behind the head, and carefully inserting a credit card or driver's license into its mouth. The corn snake will not like the presence of the card and will open its mouth very wide in an attempt to spit the card out. The mouth of a healthy corn snake will be faint blue to pink with a network of red and purple veins and capillaries supplying ample blood flow. Healthy teeth will be whitish to translucent. If you see clumps of "gunk" or "cheese" between the teeth, a darkening of the teeth, or a swelling of the gums, then mouth rot is the likely problem.

Combat mouth rot by placing the afflicted corn snake in a hospital tank and raising the temperature to a high of 87° to 88° F (30.6° to 31.1°C), with a cooler retreat of 80°F (26.7°C). While experienced snake owners can treat mouth rot themselves by carefully swabbing out the mouth with hydrogen peroxide or iodine, it is best to consult your veterinarian, who will clean out the mouth and prescribe a regimen of subcutaneous injections of antibiotics.

Pneumonia

The yellowish mass in the upper jaw of this snake is a sign of mouth rot, which can be fatal if not treated.

One of the most dangerous of all corn snake ailments, pneumonia is an infection of the respiratory tract. Corn snakes have only one functioning lung, and as pneumonia progresses, it can quickly fill this lung with fluid, killing your pet. Brought on by excessively low temperatures or high levels of humidity, pneumonia is identified by:

- Excessive and frequent hissing or labored breathing.
- Frequent opening and gaping of the mouth.
- Mucus and saliva oozing from the nostrils and corners of the mouth.
- The corn snake holding its forequarters vertically and struggling to breathe. (This is one of the final symptoms, and if your animal reaches this stage, the end is typically very near.)

If you suspect your corn snake is in the early stages of developing pneumonia, you may remedy the problem simply by increasing the temperature inside the terrarium to the proper levels. If, however, the disease is even slightly advanced, a trip to the veterinarian and prescribed medication are the only cures. Prevent pneumonia and other respiratory infections by always maintaining proper temperature and humidity levels.

Blister Disease

When housed improperly, a corn snake's belly scales will often suffer for it, turning yellow to olive-brown in color and developing a series of tiny, whitish to yellow bumps. These are the first signs of blister disease. Brought on by bacterial colonization of the skin and scales, blister disease is associated with filthy living conditions and excessively high levels of humidity.

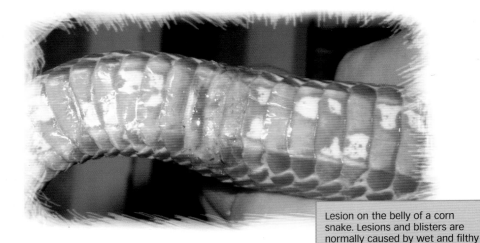

Lesion on the belly of a corn snake. Lesions and blisters are normally caused by wet and filthy housing conditions.

In its earliest stages, blister disease may only appear as bumps or discolored spots on the animal's belly. The disease is quite virulent, however, and as exposure to the filthy conditions continues, these spots will quickly develop into lesions, open sores, and pustules. The rotten flesh can extend surprisingly deep into the muscle tissue of your corn snake. Once the disease has reached this point, secondary bacterial infections will ensue, and recovery is not likely.

Blister disease is best combated by removing all substrate, sterilizing the terrarium, and moving the snake to the hospital tank. Bathe your corn snake in lukewarm water and swab the afflicted areas with povidone-iodine or hydrogen peroxide. In mild cases, the corn snake will enter a rapid shed cycle, and after two to three sheds, the cankered scales will have regenerated and appear as normal. In more severe cases, a trip to the vet is definitely necessary and is a good idea for even a mild case. Treatment will involve taking a culture, prescribing antibiotics, and possibly leaving your snake at the veterinarian's for treatment. Blister disease is serious and persistent, and many cases are fatal without prompt veterinary attention.

No matter the level of intensity, a bout of blister disease is a sure sign that the hobbyist must improve his or her husbandry standards. He or she must reduce humidity, utilize clean substrate, and change the water dish frequently.

Dysecdysis

Dysecdysis is the technical name for shedding problems. Normal shed cycles begin with the corn snake taking on a pale, bluish coloration, which clears up again about three days before the shed. The corn snake will then rub its nose on some rough item to loosen its skin at the nose. Once the loosened rostral scale catches on something (a rock, a brick, or the bristles on a large pine cone, perhaps), the corn snake will begin to slither very slowly, flexing all of its muscles and slipping out of its old skin as it goes. In a healthy shed, the old skin should pull away in one, unbroken piece, leaving the corn snake as shiny and beautiful as ever.

The tail tip is a common place for skin to be retained after a shed.

Dysecdysis occurs when the old skin is retained over some part of the body, most frequently the eyes. A corn snake's eye is covered with a modified scale (called a spectacle or brille) that can break free from the rest of the old skin during a shed. The retained spectacle will remain on the eye but is no longer a living, growing part of the snake. Retained spectacles will harden and cause future sheds to progress improperly, thereby retaining more scales during future sheds. The end result is blindness, the layers of retained spectacles quickly becoming hazy and opaque to the point that the corn snake cannot see through them. In severe cases, the eye will be so constricted by the hardened retained spectacles that it will begin to rot away, rendering the corn snake permanently blinded in that eye.

Inspect the old skin each time your corn snake sheds. Have both spectacles come off with the old skin? If not, is one still on the eye? If a spectacle has been retained, remove it by gently swabbing the eye with a cotton swab soaked in warm water. After a half hour of swabbing (which may free the retained spectacle without any other treatment), carefully pluck at the edges of the spectacle with a pair of tweezers until the cuticle breaks free. If you are unsure of whether or not your corn snake has retained its spectacle in a shed, or if you have an animal that has obviously retained several spectacles, then a consultation with a herp veterinarian or another expert is in order. Plucking at a healthy eye with tweezers and an unsure hand can blind a corn snake more easily than a retained spectacle.

The eyes of a snake normally become cloudy a few days before they shed. Be aware that the eyes get clear again right before the shed.

Dysecdysis can affect the rest of the body as well as the eyes. This leads to piecemeal shedding, rather than shedding the skin in one piece. There will be patches of skin retained on the snake.

Most situations of dysecdysis occur in severely dehydrated animals and are easily prevented by keeping fresh, clean water at your

This yellow rat snake is having a bad shed. Note the eyecap has been retained and will cause problems without action by the keeper.

animal's disposal at all times. If your snake cage or the air in your home is especially dry, you can help prevent shedding problems by lightly misting the cage once a day for a few days once the snake's eyes become blue or milky. You can also soak the snake in lukewarm water. If your snake has patches of retained skin, soaking for about an hour in an escape-proof but ventilated container will usually alleviate the problem.

Egg Binding

Egg binding, or dystocia, occurs when a gravid female cannot or will not lay all of the eggs she is carrying. This is typically due to the unavailability of a suitable nesting site. A female corn snake has natural instincts that tell her exactly where and when to deposit her eggs, and rather than deposit the eggs in an area where she knows they will not survive, she may well carry them inside her until she dies.

Symptoms of egg binding include swelling around the lower body and continual, fervent movement around the terrarium. In such cases, the remedy to the problem may simply be to provide the female with suitable laying conditions. (See Chapter 6 for instructions on setting up a nest box for corn snakes.) If the problem is this simple, expect the female to deposit her brood within hours (if not minutes) of finding a suitable laying area. If the female still does not lay her eggs, the problem may have another cause or may have progressed to the point where the uterine wall has died. This will require surgery as soon as possible if the snake is to survive. If your snake has a suitable nesting site and still seems restless and unable to lay her eggs, seek veterinary care as soon as possible.

In some instances, it is not that the female will not deposit her eggs, it's that she *cannot* deposit them. Sometimes a large or oddly shaped egg will get lodged in the reproductive tract and acts as a stopper that blocks all the eggs behind it. In other cases, an egg may die *in utero* and will begin to rot inside the female's body. The rotting egg will cause the female's immune system to go on the offensive and cause swelling, which can block the reproductive tract. If you suspect either of these scenarios has happened, you must get your corn snake to a veterinarian immediately for x-rays and surgical treatment. Untreated dystocia is excruciatingly painful for the snake and can turn fatal in a matter of days.

Providing your female snake a proper nest box will usually prevent egg binding.

A good rule of thumb in preventing dystocia is to frequently handle and exercise your female corn snakes prior to breeding them (but do not handle them unless necessary once they are gravid). A strong, muscular female corn snake will have powerful muscles and a correspondingly stout constitution and is far less likely to have problems with egg binding. Weak, sluggish, underweight, or underexercised females are much more prone to egg binding.

Signs of an Unhealthy Snake

If your corn snake displays any of the signs in the list below, it needs veterinary attention. If you are in doubt, it is better to seek the opinion of a veterinarian with experience in reptile medicine rather than to wait and see what happens. The sooner the animal sees the vet, the greater the chance it will recover.

- consistently refusing food and losing weight
- abnormal feces—runny, odd color, excessive odor, worms
- unexplained weight loss
- vomiting
- foaming or bubbling in mouth or nostrils
- tissue protruding from vent
- has blisters, burns, or other visible injuries
- inability to right itself when turned upside down

Nose Rubbing

Nose rubbing is a common problem encountered by corn snake hobbyists, and it results from using an undersized terrarium or not giving your snake appropriate hiding areas. Corn snakes, like all other snakes, need room to climb, slither, and move about. When housed in frightfully small habitats or without adequate hiding places, these animals will push against the walls, floor, and lid in an attempt to escape. The more they rub, the more abraded their nose (rostral scale) will become, and soon their nose will be a raw, bloody mess. If allowed to continue past this point, nose rubbing can eventually wear away bone; the end result will be a serious infection or permanent facial or cranial disfigurement. Treat nose rubbing initially by applying a topical antibacterial cream and making appropriate changes in your housing methods.

Burns

Burns are the result of your corn snake having gotten too near its heat source. Burns range from the very mild to the very severe and must be treated according to their intensity. All but the most minor burns require immediate treatment by a veterinarian. Mild burns may not exhibit any external signs, but the corn snake may appear "touchy" around the burn. Unfortunately, mild burns can very easily become more severe, for if no symptoms are noticed, the hobbyist isn't likely to remove the offending heating apparatus.

Mild to moderate burns manifest as spots of discoloration and patches of slightly hardened or brittle scales. These may be treated with a topical antibiotic cream until you can procure veterinary treatment. Burns tend to cause dehydration, so be sure that you are offering plenty of clean water. Burns will trigger a rapid shed cycle—the corn snake quickly regenerating the old, burned scales with lively, new flesh.

Severe burns are another matter entirely. They usually are caused when a corn snake comes into direct contact with a ceramic heat emitter, a basking lamp, or a faulty heating rock. Symptoms include severely burned flesh, deep, open wounds, profuse swelling around the wound, and extensive muscle damage. Seek veterinary help immediately; burns of this nature are an emergency.

Severe burns, which can occur in a matter of moments, are far easier to prevent than they are to treat. Make sure that there is absolutely no way your corn snake can come into direct contact with any of its heating apparatuses. Never suspend a basking lamp or heat emitter *inside* the terrarium, and always place a sturdy, escape-proof screen lid between the basking light and the corn snake.

Rodent Bites

Another of those afflictions that rarely strike the corn snake, rodent bites are the direct result of ignorance or negligence on the part of the keeper. Many keepers will drop a living mouse or rat into their corn snake's enclosure and walk out of the room. Such hobbyists do not take into account the fact that if a corn snake is not hungry it will not kill or eat its prey.

Avoiding Rodent Bites

The best way to prevent your snake from being bitten by a feeder mouse is to feed only prekilled mice. A dead mouse will never fight back. If you do choose to feed live prey, never leave a mouse in your snake's cage unsupervised. That is asking for a nasty surprise.

The other half of the equation is that mice and rats are omnivores and will not hesitate to nibble on living flesh where they can find it. When the corn snake cannot escape the nibbling desires of the rodent, the tables of predator and prey can quickly be turned in favor of the rodent. The end result of a corn snake/rat encounter can be a seriously—if not fatally—wounded corn snake. Even if a corn snake does recover from a serious rat bite, it will be physically disfigured for the rest of its life.

Milder rodent bites occur when the corn snake does attack and kill its prey. In the few moments it takes the snake to subdue its prey, the rodent will fight for survival with everything it has, often clawing, scratching, or biting deeply into the scales or eyes of a corn snake. Such bites occur frequently in nature, and wild-caught specimens often bear a great many scars inflicted by the teeth of a struggling rodent.

If a mild bite draws blood or is inflicted in a sensitive area

The tail of this kingsnake has been chewed on by a mouse. Feeding prekilled prey will prevent this from happening.

such as the eyes, nostrils, throat, or cloaca, then the bite should be inspected by a herp-specific veterinarian and given all the proper medical care. By feeding your corn snake only prekilled prey items, the problem of rodent bites can be totally avoided.

Chapter 6

Breeding Corn Snakes

In the eyes of many hobbyists, captive breeding is the ultimate challenge of keeping any species of reptile or amphibian. Many of us purchase our corn snake when the animal is at a very young age, perhaps still as a hatchling. We feed them, nurture them, and watch them grow. They mature under our care, and in time, our drive to see them conduct other aspects of their life seems undeniable. We want to see the life cycle of our pets play out to its fullest. More than that, we want to participate in that life cycle. We want to witness our corn snake mating with another of its kind; we want to see the female swell and grow with eggs; deposit those eggs; and eventually, we long to see the eggs hatch—that miracle that brings another generation of corn snakes into this world.

The decision to breed your corn snakes should not be taken lightly.

The decision to breed your corn snakes is not a casual one, however, as breeding and egg incubation are big undertakings, and the lives of the young corn snakes that will soon hatch are basically in your hands. What will you do with 10, 20, or even 30 young corn snakes once they hatch? Can you afford to keep them? Do you have a place to sell them, or can you give them to other conscientious snake keepers? Once you've answered these questions in a reasonable and no-nonsense manner and decided to forge ahead, it's time to start your breeding project. But first, you'll have to make sure your pair of snakes has all the right plumbing.

Sexing

There are several ways of determining the sex of your corn snakes. Not all of these methods are 100 percent accurate, but taken together, several methods can give you a guarantee that your snake is either a male or a female.

Tail Length and Taper

The first method is to look at the tails of your corn snakes. Beginning at the vent, the tail of the female will taper very quickly and is much shorter than the tail of a male of similar

In corn snakes and other rat snakes, the tail tapers shortly after the vent in females (below), while the tail tapers only gradually in males (above). Also, the overall length of the tail is shorter in females than in males.

size. The tail of a male will be considerably longer and more gradual in its taper than that of the female. Because male corn snakes have much more reproductive equipment to store internally, they need the extra space in the tail area to do so. When comparing several specimens, it will soon become obvious which ones are the males and which are the females.

But what if you only have one snake? How are you to interpret the taper of the tail with nothing to compare it against? Fortunately, corn snakes have a set number of subcaudal scales—that is, those scales occurring in pairs posterior to the cloaca. Male corn snakes have between 70 and 80 pairs of subcaudal scales, while females have only 59 to 70 pairs of subcaudals. Remember, when counting subcaudal scales, count each pair (the left and right scale) as one, not two. Otherwise, you might end up with an impossible scale count of 120 when the correct count would only be 60.

Probing

A second method of sex determination is probing. As the name suggests, probing involves the use of slim metal probes that are inserted into the cloaca and slid under the skin toward the tail. If the probe meets resistance and stops after passing only 2 to 3 pairs of subcaudal scales, you have a female. If, however, the probe stops only after 6 to 8 or more scales, you have a male. Because it involves the insertion of metal rods into a delicate region of the corn snake's body, probing is a fine art that should only be conducted by skilled experts. If you have

Careful Probing

Probing a snake to determine its sex is a delicate procedure. Done incorrectly, probing can cause internal injuries to your pet. Make sure a skilled person guides you through probing the first few times you do it, so that you avoid harming your snakes.

never before probed a corn snake, seek the help of a trained professional or veterinarian to show you how it is properly done. *Never* attempt probing without prior experience, as an incorrectly performed probing session can seriously injure the genitalia or reproductive tract of your snake, which can lead to infection, internal bleeding, pain, and infertility.

Everting the Hemipenes

A third method of sexing, which should only be attempted by experienced hobbyists, is eversion. Eversion (also known as "popping") is conducted only on very young snakes, usually younger than six months old. By holding the body just anterior to the cloaca in one hand, and just posterior to the cloaca in the other hand, you can push your thumb from the tail toward the cloaca to force the young corn snake's genitals into view. If one or two odd-looking pink to red stalks pop out, it's a male. If only the cloaca is pushed into view, it's a female. I can't stress enough the danger level of this procedure. There is no gentle or safe way of forcing a corn snake's genitals out of its body cavity. Permanent reproductive, muscular, or nervous system damage can be the result of eversion. *Do not attempt this procedure until someone skilled in it shows you how.* Even then, you are better off using one of the other, safer methods of sexing your snakes.

Breeding Status

Just because you have a male and a female corn snake is not enough to guarantee a successful mating. Corn snakes reach sexual maturity at around 33 to 36 inches (83.8 to 91.4 cm) long and should never be put into a breeding situation before reaching these lengths. Females that are bred too early may suffer from any number of maladies, as the process of gestating and depositing an egg clutch is taxing to her body. Males may reach sexual maturity earlier, but it does them little good, as young male corn snakes often seem to not know what to do with an in-season female.

The longer you wait to breed your corn snakes, the better, as bigger animals (females in particular) can cope much better with the rigors of egg laying than younger, smaller snakes. I personally never breed my females until they are 36 to 40 inches (91.4 to 102 cm) long. If you are breeding your corn snakes at the 33- to 36-inch (83.8 to 91.4 cm) range, it is advisable to

High-Tech Sexing

Some final ways of sexing have only recently become available. By taking x-rays of a corn snake, a skilled veterinarian can look at the results and determine the sex of your snake with high accuracy. Likewise, taking a blood sample from your animal and subjecting it to a DNA gel-run is also an excellent way of determining sex. A gel-run is a complicated procedure that basically makes a visual map of the DNA of your corn snake. Males have a certain map that is different from the map of females, and when the gel-run is complete, your vet can tell you, with almost unerring accuracy, whether your corn snake is a boy or a girl. As access to technology increases and more and more hobbyists are taking an interest in breeding their animals, the price of both x-rays and DNA gel-runs is decreasing. Either of these methods is a very safe and humane way to sex your corn snakes.

breed them only once every two years until four years have passed. By overbreeding your female corn snakes too early in life, you could drastically shorten their reproductive longevity or even their lives. Overbred females typically expire five to ten years before their counterparts that have been given rest periods between mating years. Likewise, overbred females may stop producing clutches at 12 to 13 years old, while those given rest periods may still be going strong at 16 to 18 years old and producing clutches of 20 to 30 eggs!

Prebreeding Conditioning

Because the reproductive process is so taxing for the female corn snake, she must be conditioned prior to mating. If you plan to breed her at age three (when most corn snakes will be within the recommended size range), you must spend the second year feeding her as many highly nutritious meals as possible. Feed her as often as she will accept food, though not more than two meals every six to seven days, as you don't want to make her obese. It is important that the female's body weight be optimal before she enters her winter dormancy period (see below), as she will need the additional body mass to aid her in the production of her clutch.

All meals given to the female during the pre-conditioning period should be dusted with a calcium and vitamin D3 powder. The successful formation of durable eggshells hinges on the amount of calcium the female receives prior to mating. If she has too little calcium in her diet,

the female's eggs will be thin shelled
and prone to moisture loss, fungal
infection, and will typically have a
low hatch rate. Properly calcified
eggs, however, will be ivory
white, thick shelled, and highly
resistant to molds, fungi,
dehydration, and other problems
during the incubation period.

Not only will a gestating female
need the extra nutrients for the proper
production of her brood, but since most female
corn snakes will not accept food of any kind
during the gestation period, she will need all the
nutrient reserves she can get to sustain her own life
during her pregnancy (gravidity). Underfed females that
become gravid may expire of starvation before they can deposit
their eggs—the hobbyist will consequently lose both his female and
her clutch.

It is best to wait until your
female corn snakes are at
least 33 inches (83.8 cm)
long before you attempt to
breed them.

Providing the female with ample food and nutrients during the
preconditioning period will also help her make a quick recovery after she deposits her eggs.
Underconditioned female corn snakes may suffer greatly after laying their eggs. These snakes
may stay underweight, may have problems eating or moving, or may develop skeletal
problems as a result of a taxing gestation. In extreme cases, poorly conditioned females may
refuse food altogether and expire shortly after depositing the eggs.

Wintering

In the wild, corn snakes breed in the spring. As the springtime sun warms the ground, the
corn snakes awaken from their long winter's sleep (called brumation). They drink, shed their
skins, find a meal or two, and look for love. In captivity, it is not terribly important that you
simulate this natural cycle of seasons, as corn snakes that have not been subjected to a seasonal
cycle often will breed. However, corn snakes that have been cycled often produce larger
clutches of typically healthier eggs. Proper wintering is definitely recommended for best
breeding results.

In the last few weeks of October or the first few weeks of November, feed your corn snakes a couple of large meals. Females should receive double doses of calcium during these feedings, as they will need the calcium to produce healthy, thick-shelled eggs the following spring. Allow your snakes to fully digest and pass these meals, but do not offer any more food. Once you are sure their digestive tracts are empty (about two weeks after their last meal), separate the sexes and gradually (over the course of a week to ten days) lower the temperature in each terrarium to 52° to 57° F (11° to 13.9°C).

Makes sure each snake has a hide box, dry substrate, and a constant supply of clean drinking water. In accordance with their natural instincts, your corn snakes will retreat into their hide boxes and enter a state of deep sleep. They should not be frequently disturbed during this time. It's also advisable to limit the light your snakes receive to as few hours as possible. The wintering period in nature is one of coolness, darkness, and silence. Every two weeks, you'll want to lift the hide box and examine the sleeping snake, just to make sure nothing is amiss. Remember to clean and refill the water bowl as needed.

After about 60 days of brumation (around the first to middle of February), you can gradually raise the temperatures back up to daily highs of 75° to 78° F (23.9° to 25.6°C). The corn snakes will soon resume their normal levels of activity and should be given at least seven to eight hours of light each day. Offer plenty of clean water and one meal to the newly awakened snakes. After eating, your corn snakes will very likely shed their skins. After the shed is complete, place the male into the female's enclosure.

Be Patient

Although you'd probably like to breed your corn snakes as soon as possible, you will do well to wait until the female is big enough to safely be bred. Female corn snakes should be at least 33 to 36 inches (83.8 to 91.4 cm) long before you attempt to breed them. Breeding your female before she reaches this length can be detrimental to her health.

Mating

Once he realizes a female is in the area, a mature male corn snake will not hesitate to declare his intentions. He will flicker his tongue rapidly, tasting the air and the scent of the receptive female. He will slither beside and atop her, moving in rapid, jerky motions alongside her body until their cloacas align. During this time, the female will also slither about the terrarium, also in jerky, uncertain movements. When the two animals are ready, the male will twist his lower half around the female, raise her tail with his, and insert one of his hemipenes. This is often accompanied by the male biting the female on her neck.

A pair of corn snakes mating. In this case, the male is amelanistic (albino), and the female is normal.

Copulation may last as short as a few minutes, or it may last well over an hour. Copulation may also occur several times over the next few days and will most frequently occur during the darkest hours of the night.

If you've introduced a pair of corn snakes to one another and they haven't mated, try covering the tank or leaving the room. The snakes may just be "shy" and in need of some privacy. Corn snake mating can sometimes be a raucous thing, so if you hear some banging and bumping sounds coming from the terrarium, don't worry; your snakes aren't fighting. You can put the male back in his cage after you observe several matings or after about a week or so.

Gestation & Egg Laying

During gestation, the female will require plenty of solitude and access to water. She may drink more during this period but may refuse food altogether. Nevertheless, you should offer your gestating female a meal every week to two weeks. Even if she refuses the first few meals, she may eventually need the extra nourishment and will take a mouse. Always offer prekilled items to gestating females, as the stress of subduing prey may adversely affect her or her developing brood. Expect your gravid female to stay hidden most of the time, and do not attempt to handle her during gestation.

After roughly 60 days, you will notice a marked increase in the female's activity. She will emerge from her hide, slither at all levels of the tank, nose around the edge of the glass, and may even attempt to escape. This behavior is a sure sign that she is ready to deposit her eggs. Some herpetoculturists have noticed that female corn snakes will shed almost exactly ten days prior to depositing eggs (Bartlett 1996).

A plastic storage box fitted with a lid and filled three-quarters of the way up with moist

If kept in the same terrarium year-round, male and female corn snakes are almost guaranteed to mate. Prevent unwanted matings by keeping the sexes in separate terrariums. Otherwise, you will get eggs whether you want them or not.

vermiculite or sphagnum moss makes an excellent laying box. Cut a hole in the lid of the box and place the box inside the female's terrarium. Because egg deposition is a stressful ordeal, the wise hobbyist will cover the terrarium with a heavy cloth, so as to afford the female all necessary privacy. Once she is ready, the female corn snake will slither into the laying box, burrow into the vermiculite mixture, and lay her eggs. It is smart to add the laying box sooner rather than later and to check to see that the laying media hasn't dried out.

The entire process may take several hours, and you must not disturb the female while she is laying her eggs. Once she has finished, the female may or may not crawl away from the eggs, as she will be exhausted. The eggs will quickly adhere into a clutch upon exposure to the air. When removing the eggs to your incubator, take great care not to separate the clutch or to turn an egg upside down. Place the eggs in your incubator *exactly* as you found them in the laying box.

The female will eventually crawl back into her hide box and may stay there for the next few days. Feed her as much and as often as she will accept a meal, as her body weight and strength will be low, and the more she eats, the sooner she will recover. Supplement each meal with calcium and vitamin D3, and provide her with slightly increased temperatures (5° or less), as she will need the heat to thoroughly metabolize her meals and to ensure a quick recovery.

Make sure that your female is housed alone after laying her

Female corn snake laying her eggs in sphagnum moss.

A Baird's rat snake with her freshly laid clutch. This species is not commonly bred by hobbyists.

eggs, as the movements of other females could cause her stress. If she is housed in the company of a male, he will likely attempt to breed with her again, which is the last thing she needs at this point. Once she begins to slither about and regain her body weight, the female is in full recovery, and you can safely return her terrarium to its normal temperatures and resume her regular feeding schedule.

Incubation

Incubating the eggs is simple in theory yet tricky in practice. The eggs of corn snakes, like those of all egg-laying snake species, have soft, leathery shells, which experience a high degree of gas and moisture exchange with the surrounding atmosphere. Hard-shelled bird eggs can be deposited in an open-air environment because they retain moisture. Reptile eggs, on the other hand, must be deposited in a stable, moist environment so that they do not dry out, which can happen surprisingly quickly under unsuitable conditions. Likewise, temperatures must be maintained at stable levels to ensure the proper development of the embryo inside the egg. Should temperatures dip too low or rise too high, the corn snake embryo will either develop improperly (showing deformities at hatching) or may even die. Thus, the successful incubation of corn snake eggs hinges on the stability of a warm, moist environment.

In the wild, female corn snakes will deposit their eggs under moist debris, under rotting logs, inside mulch piles, or in other such constantly humid areas where the temperatures are not subject to extreme changes. In captivity, however, we must construct artificial incubators that will satisfy all the requirements the eggs need to develop and hatch. This is done in a variety of ways.

Rat Snake Clutch Sizes

Species	Eggs in Clutch
Baird's Rat Snake	6-14
Black Rat Snake and subspecies	12-25
Corn Snake	8-30
Fox Snake (both species)	7-30
Green Rat Snake	3-6
Mexican Corn Snake	3-10
Trans-Pecos Rat Snake	4-12

Note that some clutches will fall outside of these values. These numbers represent the normal range for the species.

Glass containers (even a mason jar will work for a very small clutch of eggs), plastic storage boxes, or 10-gallon (38 l) aquaria are all excellent choices for the body of your incubator. Fill the bottom of the container with 2 to 3 inches (5.1 to 7.6cm) of incubation medium, which may include sphagnum moss, vermiculite, perlite, or even a thick layer of paper towels. Whatever incubation medium you choose, make sure to keep it moist at all times. Mix vermiculite, perlite, or sphagnum moss 1:1 by weight with water. The resulting mixture should be moist to the touch but not dripping wet. Wring it out with your hands until no more water drips out; it will still be sufficiently moist for the eggs.

Once you've procured the body of the incubator and the medium, it's time to consider a heating apparatus. The exact style of heating you choose is up to you, and a great many methods will work. Some hobbyists use aquarium heaters submerged in the moist substrate, while others place a tub of water in the incubator and put the fully submersible heater in the dish. Some use heat lamps or heat emitters set up on a thermostat. I've even had success by using no heater at all but simply keeping the incubator near a well-lit window. I personally recommend that the hobbyist place a tub of water near the eggs, place a fully submersible aquarium heater into the tub, set the thermometer at 85° F (29.4°C), and refill

Corn snakes incubating on vermiculite. The stains on these eggs did not hinder their viability; every egg in this clutch hatched.

the tub with bottled water daily. Use bottled water because city waters and well waters may contain chemicals (such as chlorine or fluorine) that may be harmful to the developing embryos. The heater will provide constant, gentle warmth inside the incubator, and by heating and evaporating the water, will create a considerable degree of humidity as well.

You will need a water-impermeable lid for the incubator. By putting a screen lid on a converted 10-gallon (37.9 liter) aquarium and covering that with a layer or two of cellophane, you can conquer the problems of both humidity and oxygen exchange in one stroke. It is critical that the eggs stay moist, so covering perhaps 90 percent of the screen lid will trap the humidity, and leaving the remaining 10 percent or so uncovered will allow for plenty of oxygen to enter the incubator. If using a plastic storage box as an incubator, you'll definitely need to cut or poke a series of very small holes in the lid.

Once the female has deposited her eggs, carefully remove them by hand from the laying box and place them in the incubator. Do not turn or flip any eggs over when transferring them, and be sure not to separate any eggs from the clutch. It is fine if some eggs are not attached to the others, but don't separate any that are attached. Place the eggs in the medium, turn on the heater, cover the lid, and monitor the eggs daily for any signs of problems. Dimples appearing in the sides of the eggs may be a sign that the humidity level is too low, while fungus or mold growth may indicate excessive humidity and poor oxygen exchange. By placing a thermometer and a humidity gauge inside the incubator, you can get a good idea of the climatic conditions inside the incubator and can make any adjustments necessary. Ideal incubation conditions for corn snake eggs are temperatures of 80° to 83° F (26.7° to 28.3°C) and a relative humidity of 77 to 80 percent.

Corn snake eggs have been hatching in the wild for millions of years and can tolerate slight variations in temperature and humidity for short periods. However, it is best to avoid any wild swings in temperature and humidity by having the incubator set up a few days ahead of time.

Temperature & Temper

Over the past two decades, I've noticed a definite trend in the temperature at which my corn snake eggs incubate, and the temper of the emerging offspring. If incubated at temperatures toward the low end of the acceptable spectrum (79° to 86°F [26.1° to 30°C] is the spectrum), the young tend to be more mild mannered, calmer, more likely to feed without problems, and easier to handle. This "benevolent range" of temperature is 79° to 82° F (26.1° to 27.8°C).

When eggs are incubated at the high end of the acceptable range, the emerging young are prone to bite, reluctant to feed, ill mannered, and are more difficult to handle as they mature into adulthood. These individuals were incubated at 83° to 86° F (27.8° to 30°C) and hatched two to three weeks earlier than their counterparts. At adulthood, these corn snakes also tend to have smaller egg clutches, and they do not attain the same body weights as those individuals that incubated at lower temperatures.

Monitor and adjust the humidity and temperature as needed. This will prevent any losses due to sudden spikes or drops of temperature.

Any sterile eggs (slugs) or eggs that become moldy must be removed from the clutch and disposed of (in the case of slugs) or removed to a separate incubator. Molds are not often fatal to the egg if they are not allowed to grow rampantly over the egg. Remove all visible mold by gently wiping off the affected eggs with a damp cloth each day until the egg hatches. Once regulated successfully, the incubator will function like a miniature greenhouse and will soon give rise to the next generation of corn snakes.

Hatching

The first time you breed corn snakes, the hatching will be a joyous and interesting event in your life. One day, you will raise the lid on your incubator and see two dozen little corn snake snouts poking from their egg shells, flickering their tongues, and getting their first look at the world. Even after breeding them many times, hatching is still an exciting and heartwarming time.

After incubating for roughly 60 to 70 days, the developing corn snakes are ready to hatch. They come equipped with a unique bony protrusion growing from their rostral scale. Shaped much like a Native American arrowhead, this growth, called an egg-tooth, is quite sharp, and when the baby corn snake moves about inside the egg, the egg-tooth makes tiny slits in the leathery shell. After making enough such minute slits, the egg-tooth finally pierces the shell, and the embryonic fluid spills out. Once this occurs, the young corn snake will poke its head out of the shell in order to draw its first breaths. When the egg has been slit and the snake may or may not be sticking its head out, the egg is said to be "pipped."

It is critical that you not force a hatchling to leave its egg prematurely. Hatchling corn snakes may sit with only their heads exposed for hours or even days before fully emerging from their shells. During this period, the baby snake is absorbing the last of its yolk sac. Only when the yolk is completely gone and the umbilical cord broken will the young snake leave its shell. Forcing it out of its shell or pulling on the young snake is often a fatal mistake. Likewise, make sure you leave the lid on the incubator during the hatch, too. I know how tempting it is to watch each and every minute of the hatch, but leaving the lid off the incubator can cause the eggshells to dry out, possibly constricting and trapping the neonates.

Rearing a New Generation

After they have fully emerged from their eggs, each baby corn snake should be placed in its own habitat. At this early stage of life, a small deli cup outfitted with a folded paper towel is sufficient. Avoid housing the hatchling on organic substrates (such as mulch or moss) for the first two weeks, as the open slit on its belly (where the umbilical cord was attached) is prone to infection, especially if the young snake slithers atop filthy organic materials. Though the hatchlings will not feed for several days, it is important that each one be offered fresh drinking water. Use a very shallow dish, such as the lid from a pill bottle, as the young snakes may crawl into and drown in a deep or steep-sided water dish.

An albino corn snake takes its first look at the world.

Within a week to ten days after hatching, the young corn snakes will go through their first shed. Known as the postnatal shed or post-hatching shed, this event marks the beginning of the corn snake's willingness to feed. Prekilled pinkie mice are usually taken with gusto, though

Get Ready, Get Set, Hatch!

Most often, the entire clutch will hatch within three to four days of each other. In other words, if the first egg pips on a Monday, the last one will likely have begun to hatch by Thursday of the same week. It is not uncommon, however, for some eggs to take considerably longer to hatch. As long as an unhatched egg is viable (plump and healthy looking), leave it in the incubator and do not dispose of it. I've personally seen a corn snake egg hatch nearly three weeks after the rest of the clutch had emerged.

some specimens have to be coerced into taking their first meal. Use small pinkies at first, and wait for each meal to be fully digested before offering the next. After taking a few meals, the hatchlings can be set up in a small cage or cages just as the adults are housed.

The eggs in a corn snake clutch will normally hatch at close to the same time, often within a few hours of each other.

Reluctant Feeders

Occasionally, you will find a hatchling corn or rat snake that does not want to eat. Generally, if you keep offering food, you will find the snake eventually takes it. To help get the little one to feed, try feeding in the dark, either by waiting for night or by putting some sort of covering over the enclosure. Feeding in a confined space like a deli cup also can encourage feeding.

Snakes, adults or hatchlings, that refuse to feed on rodents can often be tempted by a lizard or a lizard-scented pinkie. A Baird's rat snake eating a swift is pictured.

Braining If your hatchling continues to refuse food, you will have to resort to one of several tricks to entice the snake to feed. One is to "brain" the prey item. Do this only with prekilled items. Slit the top of the pinkie's skull open with a sharp knife and smear the oozing brains and blood all over the pinkie. While this practice may sound barbaric, bear in mind that the pinkie is already dead and will not know the difference, and the scent of brains and blood can turn an otherwise picky eater into a ravenous pinkie-eating machine. After you brain the first couple of pinkies, your hatchling corn snake should lose its distaste for food and should start accepting unbrained pinkies.

Bumping A second tactic is to bump the young corn snake with the pinkie mouse. Grasp the prekilled pinkie between your thumb and index finger, and gently rap the sides of your hatchling corn snake with it. This maneuver will agitate the young corn snake and often will entice the hatchling to strike, grasp the pinkie in its jaws, and begin to swallow. When it does so, you must remain perfectly still until the hatchling is finished consuming its meal, as any movement on your part may frighten the corn snake into spitting the pinkie back out or even striking at you.

Scenting Many hobbyists use the scenting method to convince their young snakes to feed. Scenting is the act of rubbing an odorous item all over the food item that you want your hatchling snake to eat. This causes the food item to smell like the odorous item. This may trick the baby snake into eating a prey item that it was previously reluctant to feed upon. Very small, hairless pinkie mice, for example, often have poor scent or low levels of odor, thus some hatchling snakes may not view these baby mice as food. By vigorously rubbing the pinkie against the fur and skin of an adult mouse or rat, the pinkie will take on an odor that is much more appetizing and appealing to the young corn snake. A similar scenario may occur when feeding snake-sausages or other processed foods to snakes that are resistant to taking the non-mouse feeder items.

Pumping A final trick for feeding a reluctant hatchling is to use a pinkie pump. A pinkie pump is a metal syringe that opens in the back and liquefies the pinkie mice you put inside. The rounded tip can be carefully inserted into the baby corn snake's mouth, and the now liquefied meal can be slowly and gently pumped down the hatchling's throat. If you take the pinkie pump route (which should always be a last resort), be sure to allow your hatchling to swallow the meal as fast or faster than you can pump it in. A liquefied mouse is not a true liquid, and you must not pump too fast, as your corn snake must have time to swallow the chunky mixture, lest it choke or injure itself internally. Always get an experienced person to show you the correct way to use a pinkie pump.

After taking its first couple of meals, you'll want to start your hatchling corn snake on a calcium- and vitamin-supplemented feeding schedule, as recommended in the feeding chapter. Now that it's feeding and functioning properly, your new little corn snake can be treated just as any other—the newest member in over 25 million years worth of corn snake generations.

Scenting With Lizards

Sometimes baby snakes just refuse to eat rodents no matter what trick you use. Before resorting to the drastic measure of using a pinkie pump, you can try scenting with something besides another rodent. Remember that many hatchling rat snakes eat lizards in the wild. Scenting a pinkie with a lizard will often stimulate your hatchling to gobble up the pinkie. Small anoles and geckos tend to work best, but almost any lizard will do. If you don't want to stress out your pet lizard by rubbing it on a pinkie, you can use a piece of shed lizard skin.

Chapter 7

The Colors of the Corn Snake

As the captive breeding efforts of more and more herpetoculturists continue, more and more color morphs of corn snakes are appearing in the pet trade. Through a process known as selective breeding, hobbyists and professionals are able to reduce some colors in their livestock while accentuating or enhancing others. The end result is a strain of corn snakes whose coloration and pattern would never occur in nature. Bear in mind that all natural corn snakes have four basic colors: black, red, yellow, and white. By fine-tuning these color ratios and intensities, breeders can create some amazing colors and patterns in their corn snakes.

The Basics

Let's begin with a little background on selective breeding and genetics. Composed of units of DNA, each gene in an animal is responsible for a particular morphological aspect of that creature. For example, your eye color, the shape of your nose, your earlobes, and the way the hair grows on your head are all controlled by the presence, absence, or dominance of different genes. For some traits, one gene is responsible, but for others, it may take dozens or hundreds of genes working with and against each other to determine the physical form. This same situation holds true for the colors and patterns seen in corn snakes. When a breeder finds a male containing a desirable gene and breeds it with a female containing the same gene, the offspring of their mating will have that gene.

It gets a little more complicated, as not all of the offspring may have the gene in question, and even fewer will display the gene in question. This is due to the fact that each parent corn

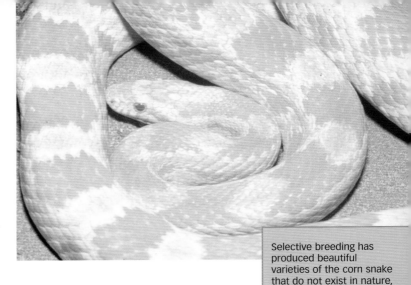

Selective breeding has produced beautiful varieties of the corn snake that do not exist in nature, such as the butter corn.

Example Cross With One Recessive Trait

	Male Gene A	Male Gene a
Female Gene A	AA Present in 25% of young (No recessive genes)	Aa Present in 25% of young (Heterozygous: Carries desired gene, but does not show it)
Female Gene a	Aa Present in 25% of young (Heterozygous: Carries desired gene, but does not show it)	aa Present in 25% of young (Homozygous: Displays desired recessive traits)

Genotype vs. Phenotype

The terms *genotype* and *phenotype* often come up when discussing the selective breeding of animals. The two terms are different but related. The genotype is the actual genetic makeup of an organism, as distinguished from its physical appearance. The phenotype is the observable physical and/or biochemical characteristics of an organism, as determined by genetics and environmental factors. Thus, the genotype determines the phenotype.

snake has two copies of each gene that it can pass to its offspring, but will only pass one. Additionally, some genes occur in two forms, dominant and recessive. A recessive gene only affects the phenotype if two copies are present; a dominant gene will affect it even if only one copy is present. For example, a male corn snake has dominant gene "A," which we'll call normal color, and recessive "a," which is a gene for amelanism (lack of all black pigment). The female also has genes "A" and "a." To demonstrate how these genes will be distributed in their young, we can use the Punnett square at left.

Each parent will give an offspring approximately 50 percent of its genes; therefore, we can see the results of their mating. About 25 percent of the young will not possess the recessive gene "a" and will not be able to pass it along to their own offspring in the future. Another 50 percent will have "Aa." These animals are referred to as heterozygous, and though they do not display the recessive trait of amelanism, they are carriers of the gene and can pass it along to their offspring when they mature. The final 25 percent of young will both possess the recessive gene and display it in their external appearance. These few offspring are exactly what the breeder wanted—corn snakes that lack all black pigment.

Of course, all of genetics is not nearly this simple, as more complex genes and gene combinations are much more involved. Experience in selective breeding and deeper study into the inner workings of corn snake genetics can teach you much more about the technical aspects of selective breeding. But putting all of the technical calculations and estimates aside, the brilliant world of the genetically manipulated corn snake is truly a sight to behold.

Color Morphs

Corn snakes are probably the most frequently bred snakes. Hobbyists and professional breeders produce literally thousands of them each year. Add to this their high variability, and

Amelenistic corn snakes that lack white pigment are called sunglows.

you can understand that there are always new morphs coming into existence. Additionally, some morphs get named more than once, and some sellers will name even slight variations in the hopes of boosting sales. With those caveats out of the way, the following is a glossary of some of the staple corn snake morphs.

Amelanism

Amelanism is perhaps the oldest of all color variations in corn snakes. In the late 1950s, selective breeding projects were underway involving wild-caught specimens that lacked all black pigment. Originally called albinos, which is taken from the Latin word meaning *white*, these snakes were not truly white. They still displayed reds, yellows, and whites. Only the black pigment was missing; the black pigment is called melanin, hence the term *amelanistic*. There are two types of amelanism known, called "type A" and "type B." If you breed a type A amelanistic corn snake to a type B amelanistic corn, the offspring will appear normal but will be carrying both type A and type B recessive genes.

Variations One of the most well known variants of the amelanistic corn snake is the sunglow corn snake, which lacks all black, as well as all white, pigment. Its yellows and oranges compose the base coloration, while the reds appear in well-defined saddles. Other forms that exhibit a primarily yellow hue (still lacking blacks and most whites, with subdued reds) are known as creamsicle corn snakes. These corns originally resulted from breeding amelanistic corn snakes to Great Plains rat snakes, *Pantherophis guttatus emoryi*. Now, creamsicles are bred to each other to produce the desired appearance or crossed with other varieties to establish new morphs.

Another form of amelanistic corn snake is appropriately named the candy cane corn snake. This morph lacks most orange pigments. With a base coloration of white marked with vibrant red saddles, this variant very closely resembles its namesake of the candy cane. Similar in appearance to the candy cane corn is the albino Okeetee, which closely resembles the Okeetee pattern (found in corn snakes hailing from southern South Carolina) corn snake, but with no

The amelanistic (albino) corn snake was the first popularly bred color morph. This particular snake is an amelanistic Miami phase corn snake.

black pigment, heightened white rings around the red saddles, and a base coloration of orange-yellow. Like a negative of a photograph, this variety is the inverse of the Okeetee corn snake.

Anerythrism

The red pigment in reptiles is called erythrin, so the snakes lacking this pigment are called anerythristic. These snakes are generally black and white with some yellows. Like amelanism, anerythrism has been tinkered with and finely tuned to produce a wide variety of unusual looking corn snakes. A second type of anerythrism—type B—occurs in the wild. This produces corn snakes that are colored in bluish grays and black. They are called charcoal corn snakes.

Snow

What happens when you breed an anerythristic corn to an amelanistic corn? Because both genes are recessive, you get normal-looking corn snakes. However, if you breed those corns together, you will end up with some babies that show both recessive traits. These are one of the most popular corn snake color variants of all time: snow corns. Defined by a nearly total lack of all red, black, and yellow pigmentation, the snow corn has enhanced white color, such that it quite literally looks like it's made of snow. As juvenile snow corns mature, however, yellow tinges

The flame morph developed by selecting for bright red coloration in hypomelanistic individuals.

often become apparent around the chin and throat areas.

Even more attractive, perhaps, than the snow corn, is its more genetically refined counterpart, the blizzard corn. By breeding a charcoal corn snake (which lacks all yellow pigmentation) with an amelanistic corn and then breeding those offspring together, the formula for the world's first perfectly white snake was made complete. The blizzard corn is 100 percent white, showing no other colors at all.

Bloodred

While red pigment is greatly reduced or absent in the many genetic variations, it is certainly the predominant color in a strain of corn snakes known as the bloodreds. Appearing as literally blood red, these corns are sometimes called hypererythristic and have greatly enhanced red pigmentation. Little to no black coloration shows, and the dorsal, dorsolateral, and ventral patterns are greatly reduced. The bloodreds may be pinkish to rosy at hatching but will get considerably darker with age. Neonates and juveniles still retain much of their natural patterning and saddle formation, while old adults take on a deep red color that obscures dorsal patterning.

Snow corns exhibit two recessive traits, amelanism (lack of black pigment) and anerythrism (lack of red pigment).

Hypomelanism

The term hypomelanism refers to a reduction of, though not a total elimination of, black pigmentation. Hypomelanism allows the herpetoculturist to create even more varieties of corns that do not display the dramatic colors of the anerythristic or

amelanistic color morphs. Instead, these animals display manipulation—not elimination—of the naturally occurring colors and are renowned for their very subtle interplay of color. Hypomelanism has given rise to such varieties as ultra-hypo, amber, and ghost corn snakes. Hypomelanism is a recessive trait and is subject to an extreme degree of natural variation.

Pattern Variation

Just as there are genes that contribute to a corn snake's coloration, there are also genes that determine the animal's pattern. These genes can also be manipulated to create a whole other wave of designer corns. There are currently only a few major subdivisions of pattern variation, but just as is true of color variations, new and more interesting pattern variants can appear at any time.

The Aztec morph is a variation on the zigzag with more irregular blotches.

Motley

Perhaps the best known of all corn snake pattern variants is the motley form. Motley corn snakes have a pattern in which the saddles have joined at all corners and washed over nearly the entire dorsal surface, leaving only tiny ovals of base coloration remaining. The motley pattern is also the most highly variable of all the pattern variations. In fact, the dorsal patterning of a motley corn snake may be as unique as a human's fingerprint. Motley corns have reduced or absent ventral pattern.

It is also not uncommon for the entire motley pattern to be broken into stripes, lines, ladder formations, or some other crude pattern along the corn snake's dorsum. Motley also appears in degrees, so a corn snake can be mostly normally patterned but have areas where the saddles run together.

Striped and Banded Corns

As selective breeding efforts continue to enhance and change the motley pattern, two new variations have occurred. Professional breeders have created the striped corn snake. This

Bloodred Breeding Difficulties

The bloodred morph seems to have several health and breeding problems associated with it. Many hobbyists complain of hesitance to feed in hatchling bloodred corns. Unlike most other strains of corn snakes, bloodreds may only feed on live lizards. Bloodred corns also show unusual variation in their reproductive habits, as they exhibit unusually large egg clutches with proportionally smaller eggs. Within my own breeding endeavors, I have also noted a higher slug rate (unfertilized eggs) among my bloodreds' clutches as compared to normal corn snake eggs. Other breeders have also noted fertility issues with this morph.

pattern is a very clean, dual set of longitudinal lines running from the base of the animal's neck to the tip of the tail.

Despite their beauty, however, there are definite drawbacks to striped corn snakes in captivity. Female striped corn snakes seem to yield smaller clutch sizes (and smaller eggs) than other corn snake varieties. So, it seems that in manipulating the genes to create the attractive striping, professional breeders also triggered some negative side effects in these corn snakes' reproductive abilities. If you are purchasing a striped corn snake simply as a pet, these factors may be of little concern to you.

Professional breeders are now producing corn snakes with broad saddles that reach almost entirely across the animal's dorsum. Appropriately known as the banded corn snakes, these animals are, in my opinion, some of the most beautiful corn snakes on the market today. These snakes may also be sold under the label of milk snake phase corn snakes, as their full-body bands are much akin to the wide saddles seen naturally in some types of the milk snake, *Lampropeltis triangulum*. Fortunately, the banded corn snakes do not seem to suffer from the same genetic side effects that plague the striped varieties.

Zigzag

In the zigzag pattern, the dorsal saddles are split apart into staggering and adjoining semi-saddles, giving a definite zigzag or zipper appearance. The dorsolateral blotches may also fuse into vague lines and zigzags along the animal's flanks. In most cases, however, the dorsolateral blotches are greatly reduced and are frequently nebulous and irregular in shape and size. The zigzag corn snake pattern, like most aberrant patterns, is not always clean-cut, and it is subject to a high degree of variation.

Bloodred corn snakes are beautiful but often have fertility problems.

Variations Zigzag patterns may have breaks in them, the saddles not touching in some places, or they may be continuous from the head to the tip of the tail. Those specimens sporting continuous patterns typically fetch the highest price. These snakes are sometimes encountered under the name zipper corn snake.

Very asymmetrical zigzag corns are currently being produced in small numbers and are popularly known as Aztec corn snakes. Aztec corn snakes are easily recognized, as their scattered, semi-fused dorsal markings are reminiscent of the drawings and carvings of the ancient Aztec people of Central America.

The exact names I apply here to designer corn snakes are generally accepted across the herp market but may vary from breeder to breeder. As a final word on corn snake colors and pattern variations, I'd like to point out that all of the above information is incomplete. As soon as this book is in print, there will be new variations and new color morphs of corn snakes on the market. The field of selective breeding never sleeps.

Chapter 8

Other North American Rat Snakes

While the corn snake is the most popular and most highly recommended of the rat snakes for the hobbyist, there are at least ten other species and subspecies of *Pantherophis*, and most of them make interesting pets. Additionally, there are a handful of other snakes referred to as rat snakes that are available in more limited numbers to the snake aficionado. If you've come to love corn snakes, it only stands to reason that you might become interested in keeping their close relatives.

Guttatus Group

In the wild, the corn snake and its close relatives compose what I will refer to here as the *guttatus* group. The nominate species of this small group is the corn snake, *Pantherophis guttatus*. Over the eons, the original *Pantherophis guttatus* has developed into two subspecies: the true corn snake, *Pantherophis guttatus guttatus*, and the Great Plains rat snake, *Pantherophis guttatus emoryi*. Other subspecies have been recognized over the years, most notably *P. g. rosacea*, the rosy rat snake, but currently only two subspecies exist.

Great Plains Rat Snake

The Great Plains rat snake is widely spread from central Louisiana and the Mississippi River Valley (around Missouri and Illinois), west to the Rocky Mountains, south through Texas, and deep into central and eastern Mexico. A small isolated population of *P. g. emoryi* also exists in eastern Utah and western Colorado.

A rugged yet demure serpent, the Great Plains rat snake is abundant throughout its range and is commonly seen crossing lonely highways after sunset. They have almost the exact same pattern as the corn snake, but they lack the bright colors of that subspecies. Wearing a base color of gray to sandy-olive, the Great Plains rat snake bears a row of cleanly defined chocolate-colored saddles along the mid-line of the back, with smaller dorsolateral blotches of the same color lining its flanks. The crown of the head bears the signature "spear-point" marking.

Prey items of the Great Plains rat snake include mice, rats, baby rabbits, and all manner of birds and their eggs. Probably owing to their superior camouflage, these

The Great Plains rat snake is the subspecies of corn snake that occurs west of the Mississippi River.

Species or Subspecies?

The concept of subspecies is a tricky one for hobbyists. It is used to mark a form of an animal that is distinct from the main form but not distinct enough to consider it a species. However, there is often considerable debate among biologists, hobbyists, naturalists, and other interested parties about whether a given subspecies is actually a species, a subspecies, or just a variant that should not be formally recognized. Although this may seem to be an esoteric debate, how things are named has real world impact for conservation laws and breeders.

When dealing with subspecies, it is perhaps best to keep in mind that the subspecies may be a full species. If you are breeding a certain subspecies of rat snake, try to breed only members of a given subspecies together, rather than mixing subspecies. Also, don't get too attached to the name of the subspecies. It's entirely possible that research will prove it to be a full species; it is also equally possible that research will prove it to be an indistinct form.

rat snakes are deft hunters of quail and pheasant chicks, often slithering to within inches of the nesting birds without being noticed. When disturbed, the Great Plains rat snake will raise its fore-portions into a striking coil and rapidly vibrate its tail against dry vegetation, making a "buzzing" sound. This display is often enough to frighten away small predators, curious cats and dogs, and most humans; in fact, an angry Great Plains rat snake very closely resembles the lethal western diamondback rattlesnake, *Crotalus atrox*. Once brought into captivity, however, wild specimens quickly tame to the touch of humankind.

Rarely exceeding 4 feet (1.4 m) in length, the Great Plains rat snake is kept and housed in much the same manner as the corn snake. It has a healthy appetite, a

Corn snakes from the lower Florida Keys are paler than other varieties and were once considered a distinct subspecies, *E.g.rosacea.*

largely benevolent disposition, and will readily reproduce in captivity. Because most Great Plains rat snakes come from cooler climates (higher latitudes or higher elevations than do their corn snake cousins), they may require a longer wintering period than do corn snakes. Winter at 46° to 53° F (7.8° to 11.7°C) for 75 to 90 days. While wintering is not an absolutely necessary prerequisite for the successful mating of corn snakes, it does seem to be a far more critical step in the breeding activity of the Great Plains rat snakes. Improperly wintered specimens may not mate at all the following spring. Gestation, egg deposition, and incubation are as described for the corn snake. General care and husbandry are also as described for the corn snake.

The *Obsoletus* Group

The largest group of North American rat snakes both in numbers of types and geographic range is the *obsoletus* group. These rat snakes are less frequently encountered in the pet trade than are those specimens of the *guttatus* group, yet they tend to be more frequently seen in the wild. Turning up in barnyards, parks, farmhouses, and backyards throughout the eastern half of the United States, these classic colubrid species are what most of us picture when we think of rat snakes. Hatchlings of most of the members of this group are very similar and also similar to hatchling corn snakes. They gradually take on the adult coloration over the first year or so of their lives.

This group includes four species: *Pantherophis bairdi*, *P. gloydi*, *P. obsoletus*, and *P. vulpinus*. *P. obsoletus* has several subspecies.

Black Rat Snake

The nominate subspecies of the *obsoletus* group, the black rat snake, *Pantherophis obsoletus obsoletus*, is also the largest of all the North American rat snakes. A truly massive individual will exceed 8 feet (2.4 m) and have a girth greater than that of a grown man's forearm. The coloration is highly variable. The dorsum

Black rat snakes are among the largest American snakes, sometimes reaching lengths of 8 feet (2.4 m).

Slowinski's Corn Snake

In 2002, a new species of snake was described in the United States. It was not a mysterious serpent that no one had seen before. Instead, it was a brown variety of the corn snake native to western Louisiana and eastern Texas. Previous to the formal description, some hobbyists and naturalists already thought the corn snakes from this area were a little different, and they were often referred to as the Kisatchie corn snakes. Work on the genetic code of this animal by Dr. Frank Burbrink suggests that these snakes are a separate species. He named them *Elaphe [Pantherophis] slowinskii* in honor of his friend, the late Dr. Joseph Slowinski. Slowinski's corn snakes have a base color of gray to grayish brown. The saddles are chocolate brown to mahogany, and a few can be a bit reddish. Some individuals are among the most darkly colored of corn snakes.

ranges from solid black (in particularly handsome specimens) to grayish-black with a dirty-looking residual pattern of rectangular saddles and dorsolateral blotches on a lighter base. Though clearly defined in the juvenile stage, this pattern becomes more and more subdued as the snake matures. Flecks of white to reddish-pink may be present between the scales. The belly is most often a freckled or mottled mixture of white and black, occasionally highlighted with pinkish-red speckles.

The white-sided, or licorice, morph of the black rat snake is the most popularly bred form of this subspecies

The black rat snake is found from extreme southern Ontario, the Great Lakes region, and southern New England, south through central Georgia, and west through Oklahoma, Iowa, and extreme southeastern Wisconsin. A powerful constrictor known for its mousing abilities, the black rat snake is known in many agrarian areas as a "chicken snake" because of its affinity for frequenting barnyards, where it preys upon chicks and even small adult chickens. Slender and sleek, the black rat snake is also adept at raiding chicken coops and gorging itself on the eggs inside. In forested areas, black rat snakes prey chiefly on field mice, squirrels, and songbirds.

A highly temperamental animal, the

Young black rat snakes have a different pattern than the adults, and they resemble the young of many other rat snakes, evidence of their close relationship.

black rat snake is seldom encountered in pet stores, but some breeders produce it. With its propensity for aggression, its dull coloration, and its frequent inability to adapt to the captive environment, the black rat snake is simply not a very desirable pet. Specialists or advanced hobbyists may find this animal to have just the right mixture of unique beauty, aggression, and hardiness to make for a well-balanced challenge in the terrarium. Captive care is as described for the corn snake.

Gray Rat Snake

A paler version of the black rat snake, the gray rat snake, *Pantherophis obsoletus spiloides*, wears a highly variable base coat of dark gray to nearly ashen-white. This subspecies retains the pronounced rectangular saddles and square to diamond-shaped dorsolateral blotches throughout its entire life. The gray rat snake averages 5 feet (1.5 m) in length. Though it does not grow as large as its black rat cousin, the gray rat snake is an equally agile and deft hunter, spending more time in the forest canopy than any other North American rat snake. Originally considered a southern variant of the black rat snake, the gray rat is found from southern Illinois, extreme eastern Arkansas, west to central Tennessee, and south through Mississippi, Alabama, and the coastal plains of Georgia, Florida, and the Carolinas.

Within its domain, the gray rat snake is the dominant predator of songbirds and ground birds alike. These snakes may spend weeks or months at a time in the canopy in search of nesting birds and their young, the snakes slithering from tree to tree without ever touching the ground. Every aspect of the snake's life can be conducted in the treetops of dense forests and thickets: feeding on birds, drinking rain water or dew collected on the leaves, shedding in the branches, etc. I have even witnessed a pair of gray rat snakes mating in the branches of a live oak tree, some 20 feet (6 m) off the ground. Like the black rat snake, the gray rat is also known as a "chicken snake" by local peoples due to its propensity for devouring chicks and chicken eggs.

Two color morphs of the gray rat snake occur naturally. The darker variant, known as the normal phase, is found in regions of higher elevation (northern Alabama, for example), and the lighter variant, which is also known as the white oak snake, has very pale saddles atop a nearly white base color and is frequently encountered in the sandy bottomlands of the Florida Panhandle and extreme southeastern Georgia. In those areas where its range overlaps with the black rat snake and yellow rat snake, interbreeding may occur between these subspecies. The resulting offspring look much like the normal phase of the gray rat snake but

Black Rat Snake Morphs

There are several color morphs of the black rat snake available. One is the amelanistic, which is a white snake with faded pink saddles. Another morph is the brindle. This is a black rat that has a gray or light brown background with darker, sometimes very red, saddles. The whole body is covered in gray, black, and brown speckles. Lastly, there is the licorice or white-sided black rat snake. This stunning morph has a gray back (sometimes with traces of darker saddles), while the sides are pure white. Understandably, this has become the most popular variety of black rat snake in the pet trade.

may have characteristics of both parent subspecies.

In captivity, these snakes require a terrarium that caters to their arboreal lifestyle. Tall quarters with plenty of climbing branches are a must. Aside from this modification, all other aspects of the gray rat snake's husbandry are as described for the corn snake.

Many yellow rat snakes bear four dark stripes on the body; their specific name *quadrivittatus* means "four lines" in Latin.

Yellow Rat Snake

Native to sandy lowlands from southern Georgia, east through the coastal plains of South Carolina, and south through Florida, the yellow rat snake, *Pantherophis obsoletus quadrivittatus*, is second only in size to the massive black rat snake and is easily the most morphologically variable of all the North American rat snakes. Dorsal base coloration ranges from tan to straw yellow toward the northern end of the range, to bright yellow, dull orange, or even olive drab in the southern and coastal portions of this subspecies' range.

The pale-colored gray rat snakes found in the Florida Panhandle are often called white oak snakes or oak phase gray rat snakes.

Not only is color subject to much variation, but pattern, too, is highly changeable. Most specimens have replaced the dorsal saddles of the typical *obsoletus* subspecies with longitudinal lines running the length of the dorsum. These lines may be broken, blotched, intermingled with broken saddles, or continuous and well defined. Such pattern variation is largely dependent on purity of bloodline and geographic local. Northern specimens' patterns lean toward the saddled-end of the spectrum, while southern individuals tend toward having a lined dorsum. Likewise, pureblooded yellow rat snakes (or especially those interbreeding with the Everglades rat snake) have cleaner features, while those interbreeding with black or gray rat snakes display muddled features and drab colors representative of both sides of its lineage.

In captivity, yellow rat snakes are hearty feeders, prolific breeders, and can demonstrate a degree of tameness not unlike that of the corn snake. They may be housed and cared for in exactly the same ways as corn snakes, with two minor variations. Yellow rat snakes are almost as arboreal as are gray rat snakes and will require vertically oriented environs. These snakes also tend to be active primarily at night, so a night-cycle bulb may be in order for viewing and heating purposes. If given access to a large water dish, yellow rat snakes may spend too much time soaking themselves and are prone to developing minor cases of blister disease. To eliminate such problems, I have found that a smaller water dish is preferable over a larger one when housing yellow rat snakes.

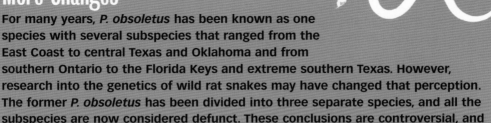

More Changes

For many years, *P. obsoletus* has been known as one species with several subspecies that ranged from the East Coast to central Texas and Oklahoma and from southern Ontario to the Florida Keys and extreme southern Texas. However, research into the genetics of wild rat snakes may have changed that perception. The former *P. obsoletus* has been divided into three separate species, and all the subspecies are now considered defunct. These conclusions are controversial, and the changes may not be accepted, but the hobbyist should be aware of the new names. The species are:

- *Pantherophis alleghaniensis:* the eastern rat snake. It is the East Coast form, ranging from the coast to the Appalachian Mountains and the Apalachicola River. This includes the black rat snake, the yellow rat snake, the gray rat snake, and the Everglades rat snake.
- *Pantherophis spiloides:* the midland rat snake. This species ranges from the Mississippi River in the west to the Appalachians and Apalachicola River in the east. It includes the black rat snake and the gray rat snake.
- *Pantherophis obsoletus:* the western rat snake. This species includes all the black rat snakes and Texas rat snakes found west of the Mississippi River.

Refer to the papers by Burbrink in the References section for more information.

Everglades Rat Snake

One of the most attractive of all the *obsoletus* group, the Everglades rat snake, *Pantherophis obsoletus rossalleni*, is also one of the most rare. While this orange serpent is bred in some numbers in captivity each year, its wild populations are diminishing at alarming rates. Growing to a maximum length of nearly 90 inches (2.3 m), the Everglades rat snake wears a base coat of reddish to yellow-orange and is accented with four longitudinal stripes, which are chocolate brown to black in coloration. In many Everglades rats, the stripes are faded and almost invisible. The unmarked ventral surface is a uniform pale orange. In areas where their ranges overlap, Everglades rat snakes and yellow rat snakes may be very similar in appearance (partly due to their habit of interbreeding), but a true Everglades rat snake can always be identified by its solid red tongue. Yellow rat snakes and mixed individuals have at least partially black tongues.

The Gulf Hammock Rat Snake

In a narrow strip of north-central Florida (Alachua, Levy, and Gilchrist counties), gray and yellow rat snakes mix and mingle, and the result is a grayish rat snake with both saddles and stripes. Locally, it is known as the Gulf hammock rat snake and was formerly considered a subspecies of *P. obsoletus*. The name for it was *williamsi,* so if you see this name in older literature, it is referring to this intergrade snake.

As its common name suggests, this animal is found primarily in the Florida Everglades and points south. Because this area of habitat is rapidly being developed for human use, however, a certain darkness has entered the future of the Everglades rat snake. Until the late 1970s, these snakes were quite common throughout extreme southern Florida, but as humankind has changed the land to suit its purposes, these snakes have been destroyed both directly and indirectly. The highly prolific yellow rat snake, which thrives near human habitations, has populated such areas in recent decades and has largely co-opted the Everglades rat snake's niche in that environment.

Fortunately, Everglades rat snakes are common in the pet industry and are widely available both in local pet shops and from online retailers. One of the most attractive of the rat snakes, the brightly colored Everglades rat snake tames to human touch far better than either the yellow or black rat snake, but it does not seem to be as long-lived. Even very old specimens rarely live for more than 12 to 15 years, which is considerably shorter than the 20 or more years the typical black rat snake lives.

As hatchlings, Everglades rat snakes may refuse to feed on pinkie mice, instead preferring tiny lizards, such as anoles and house geckos. Everglades rat snakes are highly secretive animals and will benefit from numerous hides in the captive environment. Wintering is not necessary prior to breeding the Everglades rat snake. Aside from these aspects, however, care is as described for the corn snake.

Although the Everglades rat snake is bred in good numbers by hobbyists, its numbers are declining due to habitat loss.

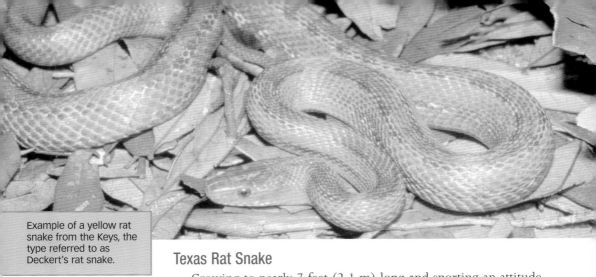

Example of a yellow rat snake from the Keys, the type referred to as Deckert's rat snake.

Texas Rat Snake

Growing to nearly 7 feet (2.1 m) long and sporting an attitude much akin to that of a *Tyrannosaurus rex*, the Texas rat snake is a great mass of serpentine muscle, sharp teeth, and pure aggression. Found throughout southern Louisiana, east-central Texas, and central Oklahoma, the Texas rat snake, *Pantherophis obsoletus lindheimeri*, has a highly variable base coloration of tan to reddish-brown or even gray-blue. Dorsal saddles are rectangular in shape and almost never touch at their corners. Unlike those of the yellow and black rat snakes, these saddles will stay highly visible throughout the animal's life. The ventral surface is a pale variant of the dorsum and is otherwise unmarked. The dorsum is often flecked with reddish and white markings, which are particularly pronounced inside the brown to black saddles. In some specimens, tawny reds to straw yellows are prevalent along the flanks. These colors, when they occur, are especially pronounced in youth and may fade as the animal matures.

Infamous for their raids on chicken coops and barnyard fowl, Texas rat snakes are easily the most aggressive of all North American rat snake species. If approached or cornered, even the most passive of these beasts will raise its forequarters into a striking coil, hold its mouth agape, vibrate its tail, and hiss

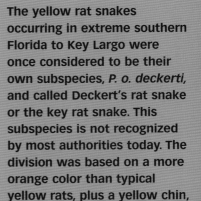

Deckert's Rat Snake

The yellow rat snakes occurring in extreme southern Florida to Key Largo were once considered to be their own subspecies, *P. o. deckerti*, and called Deckert's rat snake or the key rat snake. This subspecies is not recognized by most authorities today. The division was based on a more orange color than typical yellow rats, plus a yellow chin, red eyes, and a black tongue.

loudly. Be warned that the bluff stops here! If further provoked, the Texas rat snake will strike repeatedly and is capable of inflicting painful, bloody wounds. It should come as no surprise, then, that these snakes experience minimal trade within the pet industry—at least, not in its standard color morph.

Despite their propensity for violence, however, the leucistic Texas rats are very popular. Although it may appear like an albino at first glance, a leucistic animal is not albino. Albinos lack pigment, but the leucistic Texas rat has pure white pigment, and some of the more attractive specimens also sport ice-blue eyes, making for a highly attractive animal. To many hobbyists, the unique beauty of a leucistic Texas rat snake outweighs the animal's violent nature, which is why this color morph is bred in large numbers annually to supply the pet trade.

On the plus side, caring for a Texas rat snake (leucistic or otherwise) is quite easy. All it needs are the basics: warm terrarium, water bowl, climbing branch, and plenty of food. In fact, once you've mastered caring for a corn snake, you'll also have the skills to house a Texas rat snake. The breeding habits of the Texas rat snake are not hard to master. A short wintering period, like that described for the corn snake, should be all it takes to put your Texas rat snakes "in the mood." Gestation, egg deposition, and incubation tactics are as those described for the corn snake.

Despite their pugnacious attitudes, leucistic Texas rat snakes are popular with hobbyists for their beautiful appearance.

Because of this animal's belligerent nature, however, I cannot recommend it for inexperienced hobbyists. Anyone considering purchasing a Texas rat snake should handle an adult specimen beforehand, just so he or she can get a good idea of just what is in store when he or she does make a purchase. Buying a Texas rat snake on a whim and then neglecting it because it is so savage is unfair to both the keeper and the kept.

Hatchlings of the various rat snake subspecies are very similar. From left to right, these hatchlings are a yellow rat snake, an Everglades rat snake, and a black rat snake.

Baird's Rat Snake

My personal favorite of all the *obsoletus* group is the Baird's rat snake, which presents a uniquely beautiful collage of colors and was once regarded as a subspecies of *Pantherophis obsoletus*. Each dorsal scale is pearl and orange. Within these scales, however, another, larger pattern emerges, as the Baird's rat snake has several faint longitudinal lines similar to those seen in the Everglades rat snakes. The ventral surface is ablaze with bright orange and yellowish coloration. Hatchling *bairdi* have high numbers of dorsal saddles, usually 48 or more. Traces of the juvenile pattern can often be seen on adults. Despite its rarity in the pet trade, the Baird's rat snake presents colors and patterns rivaling even the prettiest selectively bred corn snakes.

If this animal features bright colors and a bold pattern, why is it so unpopular? Simply stated, the Baird's rat snake is native to the deserts of southern Texas, New Mexico, and northern Mexico, and it has different captive requirements than all other species of *obsoletus* rat snakes. It has different needs and leads a very different lifestyle than most of its cousins.

A very secretive animal, the Baird's rat snake spends most of its time in hiding, and when picked up, it tends to squirm and writhe, rather than settle down to enjoy some gentle handling. The Baird's rat snake is simply a reclusive, retiring animal that lacks some of the more charming "personality" traits common to the corn snake. Another possible drawback to housing a Baird's rat snake is that they are prone to respiratory infections if housed under humid conditions. Like many desert reptiles, the Baird's has a low tolerance for high levels of relative humidity, so a well-ventilated terrarium is paramount. Employing a small water dish is also recommended, as the water evaporating from a large dish can significantly increase humidity levels inside the terrarium in a surprisingly short period of time. Using a humidity gauge inside the terrarium is an excellent way to monitor the humidity levels. Ideal levels for the Baird's rat snake should be 55 to 60 percent, with as little fluctuation as possible.

Aside from its need for a dry environment, the Baird's rat snake is easy to care for. Growing to a modest maximum length of 63 inches (1.6 m), the Baird's rat snake must be provided with a horizontally oriented terrarium, as floor space is more important to this species than vertical climbing space (opposite of what we usually expect when housing most species of rat snakes). Deep, dark hides are also paramount. I have observed that the Baird's rat snake does best and seems most comfortable when the entryway

A highly orange Texas rat snake. Most individuals are not this brightly colored.

to its hide faces out into the terrarium. Place a hide box in the rear corner of the terrarium, for example, and allow the entryway to face into the center of the terrarium. This allows the snake to remain hidden yet observe everything that goes on in the terrarium, as well as in the room around it. This behavior is also prevalent in all members of the *Bogertophis* rat snakes.

Outfit the terrarium with a substrate of sand, several hides, one or two low climbing branches (sand-blasted grapevine is an excellent choice), and a small water dish. Because this species is largely nocturnal, a basking light will not often be necessary, though the terrarium should be warmed to 80° to 82° F (26.7° to 27.8°C), with a basking spot (perhaps directly atop an undertank heating pad) of 86° to 89° F (30° to 31.7°C).

Wintering is not necessary prior to successful mating, as the Baird's rat snake may never be subjected to drastic seasonal changes in the wild. A notable change in photoperiod is, however, highly recommended. Shorten the length of daylight your snakes receive to less than six hours a day for three months. Returning your Baird's rat snakes to their normal photoperiod of eight hours or more of daylight each day will likely trigger their mating behaviors. Copulation, gestation, and egg incubation is as described for the corn snake. In the wild, the Baird's rat snake may feed on small lizards during its first few months of life but will soon take rodents and ground-nesting birds and their eggs. Thus, captive-bred hatchlings may require lizards for their first few meals, but they should be weaned to pinkie mice as soon as possible. Adults seldom present any problems when it comes to feeding.

Fox Snakes

The last two of the *obsoletus* rat snakes, the fox snakes are rare, strange serpents indeed. Differentiating between the two species is not always an easy task. The ranges of the two snakes do not overlap, but this will only help you identify them out in the field.

Bug-Eyed Rat Snakes

When browsing the snake display of a pet store or the tables at a herp show, you may see some leucistic Texas rat snakes with huge eyes. Their eyes look as though they are about to pop. While some hobbyists find this cute, it is considered a defect. Usually these snakes are called *bug-eyed*. The consensus is that it has resulted from inbreeding leucistic Texas rat snakes to get more leucistics. Bug-eyed rat snakes may make fine pets, but please don't breed them.

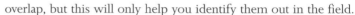

Because they tend not to do well in captivity and are becoming rare in the wild, eastern fox snakes cannot be recommended as pets.

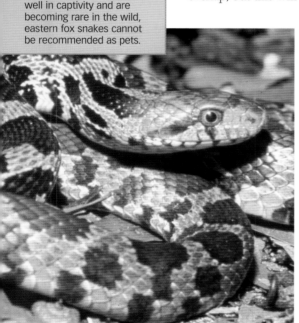

Eastern Fox Snake The eastern fox snake, *Pantherophis gloydi*, exists only in a very small portion of land along eastern Michigan and northern Ohio in the United States and in a slightly larger area in Ontario, bordering the Great Lakes of Huron and Erie. Eastern fox snakes are colored remarkably similar to the Great Plains rat snake, sporting a base coat of straw yellow or tan to sandy-gray, with darker, rectangular saddles. Juveniles have a very light ground color, and all markings, including the transverse bars across the crown of the head, are highly pronounced. Upon reaching adulthood, the head of the eastern fox snake will lose its markings and take on a reddish or coppery

Baird's rat snakes are somewhat more delicate in captivity than corn snakes.

hue, a trait that leads a great many people to kill a fox snake on sight, mistaking it for the venomous copperhead, *Agkistrodon contortrix*.

The eastern fox snake thrives only in select habitats of swamps, bogs, and other cool, lowland areas adjoining the Great Lakes. This demand for a specialized habitat makes the eastern fox snake a difficult species to care for in captivity and has certainly contributed to this animal's unpopularity in the pet trade. One of the most infrequently seen rat snakes, the eastern fox snake is simply not traded or bred in any appreciable numbers. These animals require a long, cold wintering period, which most hobbyists cannot supply in captivity. If improperly wintered, the eastern fox snake will retain a high metabolism but will enter a period of inactivity and will likely refuse food from October to the following March or April. If this occurs, the animal will not likely survive the winter, as its fat reserves will be quickly depleted. At the same time, because it will not eat, no new nutrients are entering its system. This is a common cause of death in captive fox snakes. Avoid this problem by wintering your fox snakes at 45° to 48° F (7.2° to 8.9°C) from October to late March.

The eastern fox snake is, sadly, on the brink of extinction. Its native habitat is dwindling rapidly due to land development, and the polluted waters of the Great Lakes are continually poisoning its habitat and prey items. Unless serious conservation efforts are put into play soon, I predict that this beautiful species will not live to the middle of the century. For this reason, I cannot recommend that any casual hobbyist acquire or keep an eastern fox snake.

Western Fox Snake The western fox snake is considerably more populous in the wild, and if purchased as a juvenile in the spring of the year, it can make a durable, long-lived captive. The coloration and pattern of western fox snakes are virtually identical to that of the eastern variety, though with tans and light, sandy grays replacing the

Western fox snakes are more common both in the wild and in captivity than their eastern cousins.

slates and leaden grays seen in the eastern fox snake. The range includes Michigan's Upper Peninsula and much of Wisconsin, extending west to eastern Kansas and South Dakota and south to a few spots in northern and eastern Missouri. It also includes the northern half of Illinois and the northwestern quarter of Indiana.

Most western fox snakes seen in the pet trade are wild caught, and as such, may strike and bite savagely when initially acquired. With some persistent handling, however, these snakes will quickly tame to the point of tolerating your presence. A western fox snake seldom settles to the same tame degree that a corn snake will, but it usually settles enough to enjoy the smooth, gentle warmth of its keeper's touch. If a fox snake is desired as a pet, then the western fox snake is, far and away, the better choice, both in terms of disposition, longevity, and ease of keeping.

House fox snakes in large terraria outfitted with plenty of sturdy climbing branches, large water dishes, several hide boxes (as fox snakes relish their secrecy), and superior ventilation. These snakes have also been known to thrive in large, elaborately constructed vivaria complete with circulating waterways, living shrubs, and even small trees. Even though fox snakes do frequent swamps and marshes, continual exposure to moist substrate will lead to blister disease in a short amount of time, so a ventilation fan is in order to afford excellent oxygen exchange within the terrarium.

I would definitely rate the fox snakes as the most difficult to keep of all the species in the *obsoletus* group and would recommend this species only to advanced hobbyists and zoological professionals. Daily basking temperatures should range between 82° to 84° F (26.7° to 28.9°C), with nightly drops just under 10°F (metric). Both varieties of fox snakes relish deep, dark hides and should be supplied with plenty of privacy. Stressed fox snakes have a bad habit

Fox snakes get their name not from looking like a fox, being crafty like a fox, or even from eating foxes. They get their name by smelling like a fox. When upset or agitated, they release a musky odor that resembles the scent of a fox.

of regurgitating their meals. Frequent regurgitation may cause a formerly healthy animal to stop eating in captivity altogether.

Mexican Corn Snake

The Mexican corn snake forms its own group because it is one of the few North American rat snakes that doesn't fit neatly into any taxonomic group. Also known as the nightsnake, the Mexican corn snake is very poorly understood in terms of natural habitat, habits, breeding, and complete geographic range. Even more secretive in its behaviors than the rosy rat snake, the Mexican corn snake was virtually unknown to herpetologists until the last half of the twentieth century. The hobbyist should note that if one follows the change from *Elaphe* to *Pantherophis*, the Mexican corn snake does not get placed into *Pantherophis*. This snake gets its own genus, *Pseudelaphe*. Its full scientific name is *Pseudelaphe flavirufa*.

Because Mexico does not allow the exportation of its wildlife, the Mexican corn snake has perhaps the smallest following of all the North American rat snakes. In the past, wild-caught specimens were heavily laden with internal and external parasites and seldom survived long. If an individual was successfully purged of its parasites, however, it usually made a surprisingly long-lived and durable captive. Mexican corn snakes are bred in small numbers by hobbyists.

Ranging from north-central Mexico south through the Yucatan, Guatemala, Honduras, and Nicaragua, the Mexican corn snake is thought to be a conglomerate of five subspecies and may be encountered as *P. flavirufa*, *P. pardalina*, *P. polysticha*, *phaescens*, or *P. matudai*. These subspecies are known to interbreed extensively where their ranges overlap; thus, the need for their subspecies divisions seems unnecessary. Individuals are almost impossible to taxonomically identify with certainty without locality data and will breed with one another in captivity, regardless of exact subspecification.

Though dull in coloration as adults, Mexican corn snake juveniles are quite handsome creatures. With a base color of sandy-gray to leaden, these snakes wear dorsal saddles of maroon to a reddish purple. Saddles may be clearly defined, may zigzag, or may be fused into nebulous blotches along the mid-line of the dorsum. Dorsolateral blotches of the same color are present and may fuse into the dorsal pattern as well, making for a hodgepodge of dorsal markings. Like the rosy rat snake, the eyes of the Mexican corn snake are typically alabaster white to very pale

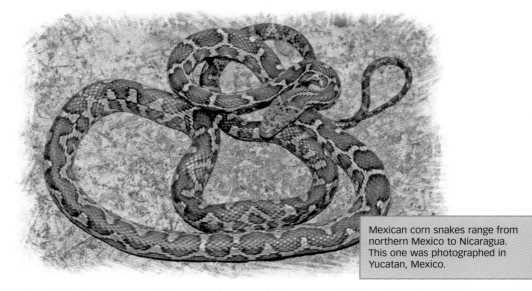

Mexican corn snakes range from northern Mexico to Nicaragua. This one was photographed in Yucatan, Mexico.

green and are highly suggestive of the snake's powerfully nocturnal habits. Though wild specimens are reputed to exceed 6 feet (1.8 m) in length, captive Mexican corn snakes seldom attain even 48 inches long (1.2 m). Captive care is as described for the corn snake.

Bogertophis

The third group of North American rat snakes consists of the species belonging to the genus *Bogertophis*. Staunch desert dwellers, these rat snakes are very different from both the *guttatus* and *obsoletus* groups in terms of lifestyle, habits, diet, and wintering. These species are also more difficult to care for and breed than their eastern cousins and are far less frequently encountered in the pet trade. If the *guttatus* species are for beginning hobbyists, and the *obsoletus* are for intermediate to advanced hobbyists, then the *Bogertophis* species are best left to experts in dealing with the North American rat snakes.

Formerly classified within the genus *Elaphe*, the members of the *Bogertophis* genus are denoted by the presence of a row of scales, which is absent in all other North American rat snakes. Located just beneath the eye on either side of the head, these scales, called suboculars, form a curved row along the lower edge of the eye and may range anywhere from four to eight in number. It is widely believed that the presence of these subocular scales is an adaptation that is advantageous to life amid the sands and winds of the desert. All members of the *Bogertophis* group also have remarkably enlarged eyes, which protrude slightly from the

Hybrid vs. Intergrade

The terms *hybrid* and *intergrade* are often used by hobbyists, but they are often used incorrectly. When two different species breed, the offspring are called hybrids. Think of a mule, the offspring of a horse and a donkey. When two different subspecies breed, the young are called intergrades. An example would be the creamsickle corn snake, the offspring of an albino corn snake and a Great Plains rat snake.

head and give the animal a bug-eyed appearance. Most people agree that these protruding eyes add an air of unique cuteness to these snakes.

Trans-Pecos Rat Snake

Found from south-central New Mexico and western Texas south through northern Mexico, the Trans-Pecos rat snake has a base color of tan to sandy brown or straw yellow. The head is unmarked but may be considerably darker than the ground color of the dorsum. The nape of the neck bears two, distinct longitudinal stripes that run only through the first two to three saddles. The dorsal saddles, which are dark brown to slate or black, are distinctly "H" shaped and may or may not touch at the corners. The center of each saddle is often peppered with light flecks of white to cream color. Irregularly shaped dorsolateral blotches occur at regular intervals along the animal's flanks. These blotches may be diamond in shape, but more commonly are a nebulous blob of light brown pigmentation. Dorsolateral blotches are typically lighter in color than the dorsal saddles. The ventral surface is unmarked and is cream to light tan in color.

Alternate color morphs of the Trans-Pecos rat snake are more popular in the pet trade than is the nominate form. These include the "blond" form, which is a much cleaner, yellow variant. Blond Trans-Pecos rat snakes have a straw to golden base color, with faded saddles and all-but-invisible longitudinal stripes along the neck. The second variant is the "silver" Trans-Pecos rat snake. Easily recognized by its silvery-blue base color, metallic saddles, and blue-tinted eyes, the silver Trans-Pecos rat snake is the rarest of all the color morphs and commands a high price among herp retailers. Both the blond and the silver Trans-Pecos rat snakes are bred in captivity, and hopefully in time, their prices will drop and their availability will increase. Captive care and breeding requirements are the same for all color morphs.

Easily the most benevolent of all the North American rat snakes, the Trans-Pecos has been described as unwilling to bite a human even if a human bit it first. While this benign disposition would go a long way in making the Trans-Pecos rat snake the perfect pet serpent

There are three color varieties of Trans-Pecos rat snakes: normal, blond, and silver. Captive-bred blond and silver ones are shown here.

for beginners and young hobbyists, the animal's delicate constitution does not allow this to be the case. Trans-Pecos rat snakes are fragile creatures that often live for only a few short months when housed improperly, and they seldom thrive under the care of any but the most skilled and dedicated hobbyists.

Care House a Trans-Pecos rat snake in a large, horizontally oriented enclosure. Use a thick layer of finegrain sand as substrate, and outfit the terrarium liberally with stones—large, round stones, as well as flat, smooth ones. Trans-Pecos rat snakes come from rocky, desert areas, and it is critical to their psychological well being that their captive conditions closely simulate their native environs. Some hobbyists have successfully employed living plants in the Trans-Pecos terrarium. Bury a potted juniper or sage bush in the substrate up to the rim of the pot. The snake will likely climb through the scrubby bush and will find it particularly useful during a shed. The Trans-Pecos rat snake will easily slough its old skin amid the stiff, prickly branches of the juniper bush.

Never use a large water dish in a Trans-Pecos rat snake's terrarium. These animals are extremely prone to respiratory and skin problems associated with excess moisture, and even the evaporation from a large water dish can be too much for this species to tolerate. Offer water in a small dish only twice each week, and never leave the dish unattended in the terrarium. All spills should be cleaned up at once. To ensure low humidity, make sure the terrarium is well ventilated.

Closed Borders

Mexico banned the export of its wildlife in 1982. Because of this, a number of reptiles and amphibians have become difficult for hobbyists to obtain. One of these animals is the Mexican corn snake. Luckily, this snake is bred by some hobbyists. It is not common, but someone dedicated to obtaining one should be able to find a breeder with a little effort. Please do not buy wild-caught Mexican corns, as these are certainly smuggled animals.

If you live in the Deep South, along the coast or in some other humid area (like foggy New England or near the Great Lakes), placing a dehumidifier in the room with your Trans-Pecos rat snakes is a great idea. Put a humidity gauge inside the terrarium, and keep a sharp eye on it. Relative humidity should stay between 40 and 55 percent at all times. If the relative humidity exceeds 55 percent, your Trans-Pecos rat snake will soon begin to suffer and display symptoms of pneumonia.

Once the problem of humidity has been conquered, the rest of Trans-Pecos husbandry is easy. These snakes are almost exclusively nocturnal and may never emerge during the day or while the terrarium is well lit. They will do well with ambient cage temperatures around 70° to 75°F (21.1 to 23.9°C) with a basking spot that ranges from 87° to 90° (30.6° to 32.2°C). Because deserts get rather cool at night, a 10 to 15 degree drop from the daytime temperatures is recommended.

Just after turning out the daytime lights, place a prekilled mouse in the terrarium in an area where your Trans-Pecos rat snake can find it. These snakes are typically excellent feeders and rarely refuse a meal. Wild-caught individuals and juveniles may only accept lizards, however, and should be fed prekilled anoles. As these animals mature (or adapt to captivity, in the case of wild-caught snakes), they will come to readily take mice. Trans-Pecos rat snakes, even more so than other North American rat snakes, thrive best when offered smaller meals more frequently, as opposed to fewer, larger meals. Even large adults, which may be longer than 60 inches (1.5 m), may prefer to take three or four hopper mice instead of a small rat at feeding time.

Breeding the Trans-Pecos rat snake is considerably different than breeding corn snakes, but still requires minimal effort on the part of the keeper. Winter both the male and female for two months at 50° to 54° F (10° to 12.2°C). Warm them gradually, and bring them out of brumation after two months. Feed both as frequently as they will eat, but do not expect the female to come into season until very late in the year, perhaps as late as June to July, or after two to three post-brumation sheds.

The eggs, only three to eight in number, will be deposited in August or September. Incubate at 81° to 85° F (27.2° to 29.4°C). Young will emerge in roughly 70 to 80 days. It is widely suspected that barometric pressure and rainfall play significant roles in the natural breeding habits of the Trans-Pecos rat snake, though the exact impact of these factors is yet unknown. It is widely evident, however, that captive breeding efforts are often frustrated or foiled by the climatic conditions of the Deep South and New England. Similar breeding projects throughout the West and Mid-West have met with appreciable success.

Durango Rat Snake

Trans-Pecos rat snakes usually fare well when housed in a naturalistic desert terrarium.

A very seldom-encountered cousin of the Trans-Pecos rat snake, the Durango rat snake, *Bogertophis subocularis amplinotus*, is considered by many hobbyists to be one of the most visually stunning of all snakes found on this continent. Found only in Durango and Nuevo Leon, Mexico, this species is protected by law throughout Mexico. Thus, its availability in the pet trade is, as of now, virtually nonexistent. I include information on it here because, as time passes, it will likely become a more commonly kept species and is certainly deserving of mention.

Growing to an (estimated) maximum length of 60 inches (1.5 m), the Durango rat snake is denoted from its kindred by having considerably wider necklines. These lines are also much darker than those seen in the Trans-Pecos rat snake. The head is unmarked, and the saddles are much more tightly grouped on the dorsum. The saddles are chevron in shape, rather than the "H" configuration seen in the Trans-Pecos rat snake. The dorsolateral blotches occurring along the animal's flanks are also larger than those of the Trans-Pecos rat snake and tend to have a triangular shape.

Baja rat snakes are primarily nocturnal, and they will generally not leave their hiding places—in the wild or in captivity—until after dark.

All aspects of breeding, care, housing, and husbandry are as described for the Trans-Pecos rat snake. If any of my readers experiences success with the captive husbandry or breeding of the Durango rat snake, I encourage you to come forward with your results, because the more accurate information that can surface about these unique animals, the sooner their numbers in the pet trade can grow.

Baja Rat Snake

The last member of the *Bogertophis* group of rat snakes, the Baja rat snake, *Bogertophis rosaliae*, is considered one of the "rarest and least understood" rat snakes in North America (Staszko & Walls, 1994). Incidentally, it is also one of the most attractive. Juvenile specimens wear a base coat of solid reddish-olive to a washed-out crimson or rosy hue and are loosely banded in thin flecks of whitish to cream color. These bands are very thin, perhaps only one scale-row wide, and fade away when the snake reaches adulthood. The most attractive adult specimens are solid rosy with no other dorsal markings, while other, duller specimens may take on a rusty-brown coloration. The belly is unmarked and sports a pastel pinkish to rouge hue. Though their natural history and habits are poorly understood, it is suspected that Baja rat snakes, even very large individuals, do not exceed 42 inches in length (1.1 m).

As its name suggests, the Baja rat snake lives only on the Baja Peninsula. Within this environment, the Baja rat snake is a prime reptilian predator of lizards and small rodents, as it is one of only a few large herps that can survive amid the scorching deserts and sun-parched outcroppings of the Baja Peninsula. Understandably, these hellish conditions have driven the Baja rat snake to a primarily nocturnal existence. Emerging only when the oppressive heat of the day has subsided, a Baja rat snake may not leave its retreat until well after midnight during the summer.

In captivity, the Baja rat snake requires a very warm enclosure that is constructed much in the same manner as described for the Trans-Pecos rat snake. Daily temperatures at the warm end of the terrarium must reach 87° to 90° (30.6° to 32.2°C). Like its Trans-Pecos cousin, the

Baja rat snake does well with a substantial drop in temperature at night.

This species will likely never bask, so heat is best provided by way of undertank heating pads, ceramic heat-emitters, or night-cycle light bulbs. A photoperiod is required for the Baja rat snake, however, as its psychological well-being seems to hinge on a definite day-night cycle. Light the terrarium for at least six to eight hours each day, and expect the Baja rat snake to become active only after the lights have been out for several hours. Methods of feeding and meal sizes are as described for the Trans-Pecos rat snake. As is true of all the *Bogertophis* group rat snakes, this species requires expert care and is definitely not recommended for the beginning hobbyist.

Senticolis

Now, at last, we reach the top of the mountain. The *guttatus* group are for beginning and young hobbyists. The *obsoletus* are well suited to the intermediate hobbyists wishing to expand beyond the basics of corn snake keeping. The *Bogertophis* are for the advanced hobbyists. And the *Senticolis* rat snake is the absolute hardest to care for of all the North American rat snakes. This animal has very specific conditions that must be met if it is to survive in captivity, and truth be told, it is one of the species that may best be left in nature.

Native to the deserts of central and southern Arizona, south through central Mexico, and throughout Central America, the green rat snake, *Senticolis triaspis*, is typically "green" in name only. Three subspecies exist and are distinguished both by their geographic range, as well as their color and pattern.

Not for Beginners

The Trans-Pecos rat snake, Durango rat snake, Baja rat snake, and green rat snake are all touchy captives. They have more exacting requirements than any of the other snakes in this book. Therefore, they cannot be recommended for the average hobbyist. Don't purchase one until you are positive you can care for it properly.

Subspecies

Senticolis triaspis triaspis ranges from Yucatan to east-central Guatemala. It has a gray to sandy-tan base color with defined saddles (45 or more in number), often trimmed in black. Dorsolateral blotches are present. The pattern is far more pronounced in juveniles and fades with maturity.

Senticolis triaspis mutabilis has a solid tan to brownish dorsum. The belly is cream to wheat-straw yellow. Younger specimens may show vague patterns along the centerline of the dorsum. This subspecies ranges from Guatemala through Costa Rica.

Senticolis triaspis intermedia is the only truly green member of the genus. It has a base color of grayish, olive drab, or even lime green. Muted saddles of pale brown to sandy-tan are often visible (with whitish flecks between the scales). The belly is a lighter green. The range of *S. t. intermedia* extends from southern Arizona to south of Chiapas, Mexico.

Nicely colored green rat snakes are stunning creatures and look like no other North American snake.

Juveniles of all three subspecies have an earth-toned base and clearly defined rectangular saddles and dorsolateral blotches. The head is also heavily marked in dark brown striping, bearing a particularly notable bar extending between the eyes. Juvenile patterning, which grants considerable camouflage to the young snakes, fades within 18 months of hatching. Adults may grow to nearly 60 inches (1.5 m), though they stay very slender even at such lengths.

Natural History

Native habitat includes rocky open lands, high-altitude valleys (to 6,000 feet [1.8 km] or higher in altitude), wooded canyons, and other such outcroppings near streams and permanent waterways. Active primarily at night and in the early morning, green rat snakes have been observed moving and taking prey at all points of the clock. There is still considerable speculation as to whether they are arboreal (as nearly all *obsoletus* and *guttatus* species) or terrestrial (as *Bogertophis*) in their habits. Reports vary, but reputable sources claim to have encountered green rat snakes both on the ground and in low trees. Suspected prey items include small rodents, nesting birds, lizards, and, reputedly treefrogs of the genus *Hyla*.

Delicate Captives

Of all the differing opinions the experts seem to have on the green rat snake, there is one thing we can all agree on: In captivity, green rat snakes present the single most difficult

Green rat snakes are infrequently bred by hobbyists. Note how the juvenile pattern is different from the adult's.

challenge of all North American rat snake species. These snakes are very delicate and must have exacting specifications if they are to thrive. Some of the most daunting problems associated with these snakes are the facts that if imported, they often suffer from heavy parasite loads and must be treated by a herp-specific veterinarian upon purchase. Secondly, the process of wintering is extremely dangerous and difficult to properly conduct; if wintered improperly, the snakes will likely die, but if not wintered at all, they may stop eating for several months (yet maintain a high metabolism) and gradually wither away. Green rat snakes are also so particular in their diet (some specimens will only accept certain species of desert mice) that they may refuse all offered items, no matter how hungry they are.

Green rat snakes are so difficult to feed, winter, and supply with the proper degree of humidity that I will not attempt to describe their captive conditions here, as no casual hobbyist should ever attempt to purchase or house a green rat snake. Anyone having the proper degree of expertise to successfully house one of these beautiful and fragile animals should intently read and reread a host of texts and articles devoted solely to the green rat snake.

In all my years of snake keeping, I have observed a definite phenomenon that occurs at some point in the lives of almost all devoted herp hobbyists. While the captive-bred corn snakes found in pet shops will always be charming in their own commercial way, there is a certain allure to discovering a corn snake in the wild. The desire to witness these animals in their natural habitat can be powerful and is not a bad thing.

Field hunting can be an enjoyable, exhilarating, and thoroughly rewarding experience. Take all the photos you want, and enjoy the corn snakes you find for all they are: wild, untamed, and ancient members of the global ecosystem. Observe, but do not interfere, and you will be doing a big favor to the future sustainability of these marvelous serpents. As world-renowned herpetologist R. D. Bartlett said, "Leave nothing behind... except your footprints and the specimen" you just encountered (Bartlett 1996).

The Equipment

All great adventures call for some specialized equipment, and field hunting for corn snakes is no exception. Before hitting the woods, you'll

Appendix: Field Expeditions

need to procure the following:

- Snake Hook
- Pocket Mirror
- Snake Boots
- Field Guide to Snakes or Herps
- Camera
- Canteen & Food

The snake hook is instrumental to any successful corn snake hunting trip. Comprised of a metal or wooden shaft, rubber grip, and bent, metal hook, the snake hook allows you to safely turn over logs, lift the corner of fallen sheet metal, and otherwise root about in the underbrush without the risk of being bitten by a venomous serpent. The truth of the matter is that a great many venomous species share the habitat of corn snakes. And since you never know what might be under the next log, sticking your hands into dark places is never a good idea. Should you find a corn snake (or any other snake, for that matter) crawling across a highway, you can easily use your snake hook to gently lead it out of the road and into the safety of the wilderness.

If you are hunting on a sunny day, a pocket mirror can be angled to catch sunlight and project it into a hollow log, cave, or other dark place into which you cannot see. A pocket mirror is much better than a flashlight, as it is very lightweight, needs no batteries, and will cast brighter light into the dark area.

As I previously mentioned, a great many venomous species (rattlesnakes, copperheads, cottonmouths, and coral snakes) share the environment with the corn snake and may be unexpectedly encountered during a hunt. These animals can bite through jeans, tennis shoes, and just about anything else. Wearing boots specially designed to protect against the bites of such venomous species is always an excellent idea, as stepping on a venomous snake can be a serious mistake. Both snake-proof boots and reinforced snake leggings (canvas greaves fitted with metal inserts that cover the shins and tops of the feet) may be purchased at hiking specialty shops, outdoor and sporting goods stores, and the outdoor department of many department stores.

A field guide to the snakes of your area is always a good thing to have, because you may encounter any number of interesting species while you are out; a good field guide can help you to identify exactly what you have found. Since many other interesting reptiles and amphibians inhabit the corn snake's environs, you may want to get a more general guide to all the herps of your area.

A camera is always a must when snake hunting, as this will be your way of "capturing" any snake you encounter. Not only will you want to record each species of snake you encounter, but a camera can be a great thing to have should you witness something truly unique in nature. I once spotted a 5-foot-long (1.5 m) corn snake hanging from an oak branch with a blue jay gripped in its coils. I stood there for 20 minutes watching the snake devour its meal. I must have kicked myself a thousand times for not bringing my camera that day!

Lastly, you'll want to make sure you bring some food and a canteen of water, as you'll find time passes quickly when you are out in the field, and you might get thirsty or hungry faster than you'd expect. Besides, have you ever tried taking a picture of a corn snake while you're terribly hungry? Your hands shake, you break into a cold sweat, and your picture is liable to come out too blurred to make out any detail in an otherwise gorgeous corn snake.

Where to Find Them

The good news when it comes to hunting corn snakes is that one might be encountered virtually anywhere within the species' established range. I've found them crossing roads, in barns, under fallen tin roofs, in my front lawn, and I even found one, a very large female,

Don't forget your camera! You'll want to be able to record the snakes and other wildlife you find.

slithering slowly across the parking lot of a local church! Typically, however, corn snakes can be found in areas where rats, mice, rabbits, and songbirds abound: forests, valleys, stream banks, old barns, the edges of fields, etc. In the height of summer, these snakes are also frequently seen crossing roadways in the hours after sunset. So search everywhere you think one might be found, and you'll definitely improve your odds for successful hunting.

Laws & Permissions

Because these snakes, as well as most wildlife in the world, are continually being threatened by the expanding realm of humans, there are a host of environmental laws to protect them from illegal collection or harassment. Violating such a law—even if you didn't know you were violating it—can carry very serious consequences, so the prudent herper will study all local, state, and federal laws that may affect how, when, and where you may search for wild corn snakes.

Trespassing is also a major concern when snake hunting. When you come creeping through a privet thicket and spy an old, dilapidated barn, you'd best make sure it's a corn snake you encounter and not an angry landowner who has already called the police. Make sure to get permission from any landowner before you tread upon private property. Likewise, state agencies and private companies may own vast, and often unmarked, tracts of pristine land, and most will not hesitate to give permission if you go through the proper channels.

Best of luck to you in searching out corn snakes, rat snakes, and other interesting creatures!

Bartlett, Dick and Patricia Bartlett. 1996. *Corn Snakes and Other Rat Snakes.* New York: Barron's Publishing Co.

Behler, J. L. and F. W. King. 1979. *The Audubon Society Field Guide to North American Reptiles and Amphibians.* New York: A. A. Knopf.

Burbrink, Frank T. 2001. "Systematics of the Eastern Ratsnake Complex (*Elaphe obsoleta*)." *Herpetological Monographs.* 15: 1-53.

Burbrink, Frank T., Robin Lawson, and Joseph B. Slowinski. 2000. "Mitochondrial DNA Phylogeography of the Polytypic North American Rat Snake (*Elaphe obsoleta*): A Critique of the Subspecies Concept." *Evolution.* 54 (6): 2107-2108.

Mehrtens, John M. 1987. *Living Snakes of the World in Color.* New York: Sterling Publishing Co.

Staszko, Ray and Jerry G. Walls. 1994. *Rat Snakes: A Hobbyist's Guide to Elaphe and Kin.* Neptune City, NJ: TFH Publications.

Utiger, Urs, et al. 2002. "Molecular Systematics and Phylogeny of Old and New World Ratsnakes, Elaphe AUCT., and Related Genera (Reptilia, Squamata, Colubridae)." *Russian Journal of Herpetology* 9(2): 105-124.

Walls, Jerry. *The Guide to Owning Rat Snakes.* Neptune City, NJ: T.F.H. Publications.

Photo Credits:

Joan Balzarini: 48, 52

R. D. Bartlett: 1, 4, 7, 8, 13, 23, 28, 30, 35, 36, 43, 49, 54, 55, 59 (bottom), 66, 84, 88 (bottom), 89, 91, 95, 96, 102, 103, 105, 107, 108, 120, 123

Adam Black: 56, 57, 58, 63, 67

I. Francais: 16, 17, 21, 27, 46, 94

Paul Freed: 32, 34, 106

R. Hunziker: 97 and back cover

Erik Loza: 24, 61, 70, 72, 74, 76, 78, 79, 82, 86, 87, 88 (top)

K. Lucas: 116

B. Mansell: 99

W. P. Mara: 38

G. & C. Merker: 11, 19, 26, 64, 92, 100, 118 and front cover

Phil Purser: 50, 59 (top), 60

Mark Smith: 104

K. H. Switak: 10, 14, 40, 41, 44, 73, 80, 98, 109, 111, 113, 119

John Tyson: 115

CLUBS & SOCIETIES

Amphibian, Reptile & Insect Association
Liz Price
23 Windmill Rd
Irthlingsborough
Wellingborough NN9 5RJ
England

American Society of Ichthyologists and
Herpetologists
Maureen Donnelly, Secretary
Grice Marine Laboratory
Florida International University
Biological Sciences
11200 SW 8th St.
Miami, FL 33199
Telephone: (305) 348-1235
E-mail: asih@fiu.edu
www.asih.org

Society for the Study of Amphibians and
Reptiles (SSAR)
Marion Preest, Secretary
The Claremont Colleges
925 N. Mills Ave.
Claremont, CA 91711
Telephone: (909) 607-8014
E-mail: mpreest@jsd.claremont.edu
www.ssarherps.org

VETERINARY RESOURCES

Association of Reptile and Amphibian
Veterinarians
P.O. Box 605
Chester Heights, PA 19017
Phone: (610) 358-9530
Fax: (610) 892-4813
E-mail: ARAVETS@aol.com
www.arav.org

RESCUE AND ADOPTION SERVICES

Petfinder.com
www.petfinder.org

Reptile Rescue, Canada
www.reptilerescue.on.ca

WEB SITES

Center for North American Herpetology
www.naherpetolgy.org

Cornsnakes.com
www.cornsnakes.com/forums

Cornsnake Morph Guide
www.cornguide.com/home.htm

Kingsnake.com
www.kingsnake.com

Reptile Forums
http://reptileforums.com/forums